RING OUZELS
OF THE
YORKSHIRE DALES

IAN APPLEYARD

All photographs by the author

ISBN 0 901286 40 0

PRINTED AND PUBLISHED IN GREAT BRITAIN BY
W. S. MANEY & SON LTD, HUDSON ROAD, LEEDS LS9 7DL

*My constant companion in the field
throughout this study has been my wife Philippa.
Without her sharp eyes, encouragement, forbearance
and help it would never have been completed.
To her this book is dedicated with all my love.*

Acknowledgements

We are deeply indebted to the various landowners, farmers, shepherds and gamekeepers who have so generously helped us throughout our study. We would like to thank them most sincerely for their co-operation.

Thanks are also due to Richard Ranft of the British Library of Wildlife Sounds, National Sound Archive for the production and interpretation of sonagrams, to Richard Margoschis for technical advice on sound recording and to the late Sir Malcolm Wilcox for tracking down other published work on the Ring Ouzel in the early days of the study.

Finally, the complete manuscript has been typed and retyped many times by Pat Perry with assistance from her husband John on word processing and computer layouts. Thank you for your good-humoured and unselfish contribution throughout.

Contents

Preface

Originally it was my intention to publish the results of my Ring Ouzel research in a paper for one of the ornithological journals. But as the field work progressed more and more people expressed an interest in the project. They were not bird watchers but were intrigued that anyone would wish to spend so much time trying to unravel the story of just one species. For my part I wanted to make a worthwhile contribution to the knowledge of birds. I decided therefore to write a book in a form which hopefully would be of interest to the country lover as well as the ornithologist. The early chapters have the first group of readers very much in mind and I have tried to meet the requirements of the professionals later on. Above all I wanted the book to be illustrated with my own colour photographs in a way which would be both visually attractive and informative.

In other words I have tried to cater for two quite different readerships. I hope that each will find something in these pages that they did not know previously about the Yorkshire Dales and some of the birds to be found there.

Flying machines

The big event of the year at Ian Appleyard's preparatory school was Speech Day. On the occasion of his first one at the age of eight his task was to recite 'Flying Machines' by the Little Stint. It made such a lasting impression on his young mind that today he can still remember every word of it. He wishes to share it with those who may, like himself, still wonder at the great mystery of migration and the magic of the world of birds.

When Bleriot the Channel flew
The people made a great to-do;
They came in thousands just to stare
At the great Conqueror of the Air
Who crossed from France to England's shore,
A flight of twenty miles or more.
'How great an aeroplane!' they said;
'And what a noise the engine made!'
'And how could Bleriot know that he
Would find his way across the sea,
Which none had ever flown before?'
And so they wonder more and more,
Until at last their hats they raise
And cheer to their great hero's praise.
Yet I, when called to make my flight,
Have slipped off in an Arctic night
And lightly flown o'er land and sea,
The only engine carrying me
My heart, no bigger than a shilling,
Which for twelve thousand miles is willing.
Less than two ounces is my weight,
No petrol cans increase my freight;
No chart nor compass 'neath my eyes
To mark the track through trackless skies —
And still untiring to the verge
Of Australasian ocean's surge
From north Siberia's coast I fly,
Spanning the globe unerringly.
No cheering thousands when I land,
No startling posters in the Strand;
No wondering word, no praise is heard,
But then — I only am a bird.

Short-eared Owl

Dipper's nest in the lower valley

Dipper

Introduction

In 1935 when I was 12 years of age my father said, 'Ian, instead of simply making notes about all the nests you find, why don't you pick one species and find out more about it than anyone else?' At the time I thought this was rather a tall order. I had just won the ornithology prize at my prep school, Earnseat, which was situated in a bird-rich area at Arnside on Morecambe Bay. It had a wonderful headmaster, Jimmy Barnes. He and my father were both great lovers of the countryside and both had encouraged my early interest in birds. As a result I had produced an annual bird diary of my finds and sightings from a very early age.

The idea of specialising appealed to me at once — but on what sort of bird? My first thought was Owls because they were included in the Appleyard family crest and were clearly an intriguing species to study. But although we always found a number of nests each year they were often difficult to reach. As a result my elder brother Geoffrey and I had frequently been caught in incriminating circumstances up large trees on private land.

The Dipper, or Water Ouzel, was finally selected as it is a lovable bird which always nests by clear, fast-flowing water. The River Wharfe, by which we lived in those days, provided ideal sites for this species on and under its many stone bridges and by the waterfalls on both the main river and its side-streams. So it was decided to make the study area the River Wharfe and its tributaries, from Bolton Abbey up to the source near Beckermonds amidst the higher fells.

By 1940 I was getting to know as individuals many of the adults which I had caught and ringed in their domed mossy nests. One bird nested for five consecutive years in exactly the same place by a waterfall near Appletreewick. I also ringed its young each year and finally caught one of them on its own nest on a bridge about 2 km away.

As I write this in my study 50 years later, I am looking at a framed map of Upper Wharfedale hand-drawn in 1940. It shows that in that year there were about 45 nests above Bolton Abbey, and that at the top end of the dale where the river is relatively narrow the average territory length of a pair was just over 1 km.

But then came the war and service in the army. Afterwards there were many sporting diversions — tennis, ski-racing and international rally driving — quite apart from the need to help my father in the family firm. (Tragically, my brother had been killed in the SAS after being decorated three times.) So although I maintained my general interest in birds there was no time to continue the Dipper study.

But one day in 1973 my wife and I were motoring up Coverdale when a strange bird flew across the bonnet. It looked like a Blackbird with a white gorget. We stopped and watched it for a while. It eventually led us to its nest, containing four large feathered young completely hidden behind a clump of bracken on a steep bank below the road. We had seen our first Ring Ouzel. My interest in this uncommon bird was immediately aroused and I vowed that when time permitted I would once again follow my father's original advice: 'Pick a species and find out more about it than anyone else.'

In '78 it was possible to commence the study. Now with hundreds of days of field work and thousands of miles of motoring behind us, this book has been written. I hope you enjoy reading it as much as we have enjoyed getting to know the Ring Ouzel.

Ring Ouzel (male)

An older female Ouzel (upper) can easily be confused with the male (lower)

Summary of the Ring Ouzel study

Over a 15-year period in the Yorkshire Dales the territories of 353 pairs of Ring Ouzels were investigated and statistical details of 164 occupied nests recorded.

Histograms showing 93 first egg dates indicate that the laying season is much longer than generally appreciated. Precise incubation and nestling periods have been calculated showing a mean for the former of 12.8 days and a spread for the latter from 12–14 days depending on disturbance.

It was noted that the gorget of a female Ouzel gets progressively creamier year by year. By the third season they can become so white as easily to be confused with a male in bad light. This change in appearance in later years has not been mentioned by any other observer or in any reference book. In the author's view it has caused a number of incorrect male/female identifications to be made by those not familiar with the species.

A particular study was made of the incidence of double brooding, which is shown to be much more common than previously recognised. The best season produced a proportion of 73 per cent with two pairs additionally raising successful third broods — an event not previously recorded. Details are given of the time intervals between double broods and also the linear distance between them.

Behaviour at the nest was studied both by personal observation from the hide and by analysing tapes taken at a number of different locations with an unmanned video camera. The effect on feeding rates of different climatic and environmental conditions is shown.

A detailed examination of the most densely populated part of the study area shows that in one particular year there were seven nests in an area of only 0.5 km². Nests were between 140–200 m apart. Density figures are compared with those made elsewhere by other observers.

Predation is shown to vary greatly from one season to another depending largely on the amount of time that gamekeepers can devote to the control of predators. The usual rate of lost nests is about 20 per cent but in the worst year this rose to 62 per cent.

Display and courtship are described and a most unusual and aggressive fight between two females for possession of a male. In published literature copulation has been described only once but in this study four separate occasions have been recorded — the last in great detail from a range of only 15 m.

The various calls of the Ring Ouzel are covered and also methods of recording and producing sound spectrograms. In the most densely populated part of the study area some of the males seem to produce harmonic variations in about 30 per cent of their phrases. This is demonstrated in sonagrams. A local dialect appears to exist in the valley which is not present elsewhere in the Dales.

Waiting at the top of the valley for the first Ouzel

The study area

Starting with no personal knowledge of the subject, the first problem was to locate the best breeding areas reasonably accessible from home. Clearly many visits would be required during the course of each year and it was desirable to minimise the motoring and maximise the hours of field work each day. These requirements produced an initial area of approximately 500 km², with its furthest point about 70 km away by road from my home in Harrogate. It included parts of Airedale, Wharfedale, Nidderdale and Wensleydale, together with many of their side dales. For five years this area was covered in a general way although the outer boundaries were gradually brought nearer home to reduce the time spent motoring. Very slowly we built up our knowledge of the habits and distribution pattern of the Ouzels.

Eventually it became clear that there were two particularly favoured valleys. Both these seemed to provide what the birds needed to flourish and what we required to study a closed community of Ouzels within a relatively small area. Unfortunately, one of the valleys had a minor road through its whole length. Although little used by the public in the early years, the amount of traffic gradually increased until at weekends and holidays the picnicking families with children and dogs were definitely having an adverse effect on all the wildlife.

Consequently in '84 we decided to concentrate our efforts on the other fruitful valley. This had two great advantages. The public had no right of access to it with vehicles and it was also nearer home. This final area for detailed study is covered by just 14 adjoining kilometre squares of the Ordnance Survey.

In the 15 seasons since we commenced our study we have located and investigated the territories of 353 pairs of Ring Ouzels and found 164 occupied nests. Of these 219 pairs and 136 nests have been in the detailed study area. In the valley the best year for total occupied nests was '91, with 21 including second and third broods. The best year for occupied territories was '88, with 24 pairs of Ring Ouzels. In '79, the first year that we discovered this valley, we located only five territories. The benefits of specialisation are well illustrated by these figures.

The lower valley starts as a rocky gorge with a few trees and a typical Dipper stream spilling rapidly down amongst moss-covered boulders. The lowest Ouzel nest found was in this section at an altitude of 250 m. At about 260 m the gorge opens out into the middle

Ouzel's nesting site in Karst scenery

Small shakehole in the upper valley

valley, which is a typical limestone area of stone-walled grass fields, gullies and crags, bracken-covered hillsides and some disused lead mines and spoil heaps. At about 350 m this terrain gives way to rough grazing land and then to the heather moors. This whole area is one where streams appear and disappear down sinks in the limestone pavement and in dry weather travel for long distances underground. In geological terms it is known as Karst scenery.

Another unusual feature is the number of shakeholes at the higher levels. Some of these are as much as 100 m in diameter and 20 m deep. They have been created naturally by the effects of water erosion on faults in the limestone rocks and are sometimes called swallow-holes or dolines. Often small streams flow into them, go underground and emerge perhaps a kilometre or more away in a lower part of the valley. Their steep heather and bilberry covered sides provide ideal sheltered nesting sites for the Ouzels on the higher moorland. Our highest nest was in a shakehole at 490 m.

The commonest nesting species are Meadow Pipit, Wheatear, Lapwing, Curlew, Golden Plover and Grouse. The least common birds observed include Peregrine Falcon, Hen Harrier, Merlin, Buzzard, Short-eared Owl and a solitary Golden Eagle. Details of the relationship between Ring Ouzels and other species are discussed later.

Throughout this book all observations on the behaviour of Ring Ouzels and their nesting habits have been made personally within the defined study area. Where appropriate, comparisons have been made with other published data from different parts of the British Isles and acknowledgements and references are contained in later pages.

The name Yorkshire Dales should perhaps be defined in more detail. *Chambers Dictionary* describes a dale as the low ground between hills or the valley through which a river flows. On the eastern slopes of the Pennines there are numerous dales with uplands and moorlands separating them and the whole area is collectively called the Yorkshire Dales. The central part is designated a National Park. Our study area could correctly be described as being upland and moorland, although for convenience I refer to it as our valley. (The Yorkshire Dales must not be confused with the North York Moors National Park, which lies further east nearer the coast and north of Helmsley and Pickering.)

The Ring Ouzel
(*Turdus torquatus*)

The Ring Ouzel, or Mountain Blackbird, is a member of the Thrush family (*Turdidae*), of which five others are to be found in Britain — Blackbird, Song Thrush, Mistle Thrush, Fieldfare and Redwing. But our Ring Ouzels are summer visitors and leave our shores in the autumn for the warmer climates of southern Spain and North Africa. The bulk of our Fieldfares and Redwings are winter visitors. They arrive from Scandinavia in the autumn, return there in the spring and only a few remain throughout the year and nest.

I have used the term 'our Ring Ouzels' because there are other Ring Ouzels in the British Isles in the spring and autumn which are birds of passage. They have also wintered near the Mediterranean but are on their way to their breeding grounds in Norway, Sweden and Finland. Analysis by Roger Durman of Ouzels passing through the bird observatories round our coasts revealed peak numbers of birds on the East Coast weeks after ours had flown in from France and started nesting. These passage migrants were recorded at Dungeness, Gibraltar Point, Spurn Head and Fair Isle, from whence they went east across the North Sea. The birds look exactly like ours. There is another race called the Alpine Ring Ouzel (*Turdus alpestris*), which nests mainly in Switzerland, Austria, Germany and France. They differ slightly in plumage from our birds but nearly always nest in trees, like Fieldfares, whereas ours nest predominantly on the ground.

In appearance and behaviour the Ring Ouzel is most nearly like the Blackbird. But the male has a white gorget very obvious from the front but invisible when the bird is viewed directly from behind. The bill is yellow with a brown tip, compared with the Blackbird's golden bill. A very confusing feature is that in some lights at a distance the bird appears black but the same bird can look brown when flying away from one. Again depending on the direction of the light both sexes have pronounced lighter patches on the folded wings. At close range the male bird is not black at all. Its breast feathers are fringed with a greyish white outer line which produces a scaly effect and can best be appreciated in a photograph.

The female is a more brownish bird in the same way that applies to Blackbirds. But whereas male Ouzels are very similar to each other, the colouring of the females varies enormously. Some have brown mottled breasts with narrow muddy cream gorgets. These are first-year birds whose plumage has developed from their juvenile appearance. Others have darker breasts with much larger and creamier gorgets. These are second and later year birds. The change in plumage starts to occur at the first complete moult in the August after the year in which the birds hatched. The gorget seems to get whiter at each annual moult thereafter.

The older female can very easily be mistaken for a male and in the early years of this study it was frequently thought that two males were being observed when in fact they were a pair. This problem is particularly acute at the start of the season, when the males usually arrive one to two weeks before the females. As many as four males have been observed feeding together shortly after arrival and before they have separated to start laying claim to their own territories. It can therefore sometimes be difficult in bad light to

Ouzel or Blackbird? The wings provide the clue

Ouzel (male)

Ouzel (female)

be certain one is in fact watching a pair and so determine precisely the arrival date of the first female, unless she is one of the younger birds with a narrow, muddy cream gorget.

When defending large nestlings and fledglings the female is usually more aggressive than the male and will sometimes strike an intruder with wings or feet. They also sometimes puff out the feathers on their gorget to make themselves look more threatening to a predator.

Ouzels are an upland and montane species with their most favoured areas in Britain being the Pennines, Lake District and the higher parts of Scotland and Wales. They nest at or above the treeline which in North Yorkshire lies at about 250 m.

So how many Ouzels are there? The *Atlas of Breeding Birds in Britain and Ireland* was the result of a detailed field study of all the Ordnance Survey 10 km squares and was organised over the five years 1968–1972 by the British Trust for Ornithology (BTO). From this survey Sharrock estimated that there were 8,000–16,000 pairs of Ouzels in Britain and Ireland. To put this into perspective he estimated there were over seven million pairs of Blackbirds.

A *new Atlas* has recently been published covering the years 1988–1991. In this the Ouzel figures have been revised downwards to 5,680–11,360 pairs. I think that even this estimate of the Ouzel population is high and that the lower figure of the range is the most likely.

Whichever may be the correct figure, Ring Ouzels are scarce and sadly seem to be declining in number.

Ouzel (f) threatening a predator

Fieldfare

Redwing

Ouzel anecdotes

The Ouzel that crossed the road

On 25 May '79 I was returning on the A59 from a business conference in Blackpool towards Harrogate. Between Bolton Abbey and Blubberhouses a male Ouzel flew across the road just in front of me and disappeared towards some old farm buildings on the edge of the moor. I hurriedly parked the car and followed on foot up a nearby farm track. The Ouzel was on the roof of an empty barn at the top end of the farmyard. I quickly located a new but empty nest about 2 m above the ground in a ventilation hole in the barn wall with an old nest in the adjacent hole. The young had obviously just flown and were on a wall and in the heather alongside the barn. They were being fed by both the male and the female.

All this had taken some time and I suddenly had the strange feeling that someone was watching me. I turned to find a farmer

Ouzel (m)

Ouzel (f)

leaning on his shepherd's crook, cap tilted at a jaunty angle and regarding me with what can only be described as a quizzical expression. Standing there in my business suit with my black shoes now covered in mud and manure I felt somewhat vulnerable. I explained that I was making a study of Ring Ouzels and had seen one cross the road in front of me. There wasn't time to seek anyone's permission to follow it and here I was. I showed him the nest and young nearby and then stopped talking. He eyed me for a few moments and then said, 'I've never heard such a daft story in my life so it must be true.' We have been firm friends with Peter and his family ever since and he has helped us in our Ouzel study on many occasions.

One particular Sunday evening quite late I was with my son and tried to drive the Range Rover through a very narrow gateway and then up and across a steep grassy slope. It had been raining and suddenly we began to slide sideways and ended up without damage but hard up against the wall. My son thought it was hilariously funny because he had been driving previously and I had insisted on taking over for this difficult bit in case he got us stuck! There was no way we could extricate the vehicle unaided so we walked about 5 km to Peter's farm to get help. He cheerfully turned out in the gathering darkness with his tractor and hauled us off the wall until we could regain traction.

By this time my wife, waiting at home, had assumed the worst and imagined her son and husband trapped inside an overturned vehicle in some unknown and remote place on the moors. We were not particularly well received!

The Ouzel in the Alpine churchyard

The Winter Olympics of '48 were held in St Moritz. I had learned to ski at the age of eight in the neighbouring village of Pontresina and was one of a group of pre-war skiers invited to train in Switzerland with a view to representing Britain. After competing in the Downhill and Slalom races I decided to relax by returning to Pontresina to do some ski-touring and climbing.

The chief guide and head of the ski school at that time was Simon Rahmi, who had taught me to ski so many years before. He took a group of us for a magical week in the high mountains during which we climbed Piz Palu (3,500 m) and many others. (During a similar spring tour before the war, my father had once asked Simon why there were no sheep in the Alpine meadows. 'Why do we need sheeps in Switzerland?' he had replied. 'We have no sea.')

In mid-June '81, wrongly assuming that the Yorkshire Ouzel season had finished, we went for a Continental motoring holiday. I wanted my wife to see the beautiful Engadine scenery and alpine flowers. We decided to

Gentians

make our base in Pontresina. As we drove up the only street in the village towards our hotel, we noticed a Blackbird feeding on a small triangle of grass outside the church. As we drew level with it and at a range of only about 5 m it turned to face us. But this was no Blackbird. It was a beautiful male Alpine Ring Ouzel with a dazzling white gorget! It disappeared up the hillside between some houses, leaving us truly astounded.

That evening in the hotel we asked the concierge about my old friend Simon, whom we wished to see. 'Alas,' he said, 'he was killed only a few years ago by a secondary avalanche whilst leading other guides to the rescue of a buried skiing party.' We were greatly saddened by this news and early next morning made our way up the slopes behind the village to the little graveyard to pay our respects to my old friend. As we were searching for the grave I saw my wife waving urgently from the far side and could hear the *chak-chak* alarm call of a Ring Ouzel. We soon spotted a cat amongst a pile of logs nearby being attacked by a female Ouzel. We chased

away the predator and then to our amazement the bird came towards us and landed silently alongside us on the branch of a fir tree, where it remained quite calm. It seemed to know we were friends.

We located the nest about 5 m up the tree at the junction of a branch and the main stem. As I was unable to climb to it we returned that evening with a ladder but the young had flown. They were being looked after by the parents nearby. As a bonus we also watched a Black Redstart feeding young in a hole under the eaves of a chalet.

As darkness began to fall we bade farewell to Simon, rejoicing that he had found such tranquillity looking out over his beloved Roseg valley towards the icy cliffs of Piz Bernina, now turning pink in the last rays of the setting sun.

The Ouzel that stayed behind

On 16 November '91 Mr Percy Lister of Chellow Dene, Bradford saw what he identified from a bird book as a Ring Ouzel in his garden. By great good fortune I heard about this bird within a week but thought it was more likely to be an albino Blackbird than a Ring Ouzel which, by this date, should have been in North Africa.

Albino Blackbird

On 27 November I was able to visit Mr Lister and, through a window, he showed me the bird feeding on the berries of a Cotoneaster growing on a wall behind his house. The range was only about 5 m and there was no doubt at all that the bird was a female Ring Ouzel, although she had a remarkably deep

The Ouzel that stayed behind

and light coloured gorget. She was probably about three years old. It was also regrettably clear that she had lost her tail and some feathers from one wing. However, she was quite agile and able to fly up into the Leylandii trees at the end of the garden where she sat in the sun on the roof of a feeding table. She apparently had a full tail when first observed but lost it, probably to the neighbour's cat, on about 20 November.

During her first three days in the garden she appeared weak and she was harried by a pair of Blackbirds. But after feeding on the many varieties of berries available she herself became more aggressive and drove them off.

She was last seen by Mr Lister on 29 November but whether the cat finally got her or she moved on voluntarily to find more food is unknown. Why she remained in Yorkshire so late in the season is a mystery. According to Mather there have only been three other cases recorded this century of later Ouzels in Yorkshire — Lower Barden Moor from 27 November to 4 December '76, Burbage Moor from 16 November to 9 December '79 and one in Colsterdale on 6 December '82. The nearest probable breeding area for Ouzels is about 8 km west of where we saw her and it seems likely that she was driven into the outskirts of a large city because of shortage of food in her normal habitat.

During the four hours that I was privileged to watch her at close range, I was able to take numerous photographs using both colour print film and transparencies, and both 500 mm and 1,000 mm lenses. I also obtained a very satisfactory video tape record of this most unusual incident.

The Ouzel that died

On 25 May '86 we found a female sitting on a nest with five eggs in a crack about 2 m above the ground at Lower Crag. We had been observing adults there continuously since 19 April and it is almost certain that this was a replacement for an earlier nest predated (i.e. destroyed by a predator) before we could locate it.

On 21 June the nest was empty but undamaged and there were fresh droppings on the rocks around that seemed to indicate that the young had very recently flown.

But, immediately below the nest on the grass lay a dead female Ouzel on her back. Her plumage was perfect, she was completely undamaged and quite fresh with no smell at all. We took her home and put her in a refrigerator whilst deciding what to do. We assumed that she had either picked up poison in some form or another, or had died from some physical failure, as she was painfully thin with her breastbone very prominent. She looked emaciated.

Red Grouse (m)

On 23 June we took her to the Ministry of Agriculture, Fisheries and Food at Lawnswood, Leeds and asked if they could determine the cause of death. In due course I received a very full report of a post-mortem examination which stated categorically that the cause of death was definitely not due to any traceable chemical. Nor was it caused by the failure of one of her internal organs. They pointed out that the bird weighed only 50 gm, which is well below the mean weight for a Ring Ouzel of 112 gm and also below the weight range for this species.

Their conclusion was that the bird had starved to death. From 14–17 June there was a heatwave and the temperature in the narrow valley at the Lower Crag was excessive at times. There were five young to feed instead of the usual four and there was probably a shortage of readily available earthworms in the exceptionally hot and dry conditions. It seems probable that the female gave priority to the needs of her young and neglected herself to the point where exhaustion and starvation caused her death. (I learned later from a gamekeeper that this phenomenon is also known amongst female Grouse with large broods to feed in hot and dry weather.)

Ouzels and aircraft

The whole of the valley and surrounding hills lie in an area of North Yorkshire used for training pilots in the art of low flying. Often from the higher nesting sites one is actually looking down on to the top of the wings as a Tornado screams past in the valley. When they pass overhead the effect on the human ear is quite shattering, and many times when in a hide and unable to see them coming I have been caught unawares. They travel so fast that one cannot hear them approaching — only as they pass over and recede. One would imagine that they would terrify the birds. But watching Ouzels at close range from a hide they do not react at all. Perhaps they think it is thunder.

But a helicopter is a very different matter. Immediately one appears overhead all the birds, including the Ouzels, dash for cover. With its rotating blades and flickering appearance, I believe that they equate it with a bird of prey like a Kestrel. Whatever the reason, the whole grouse moor goes quiet and appears deserted when one appears.

Ouzels in the snow

On 25 April '81 nine inches of snow fell in Harrogate and completely destroyed the famous Spring Flower Show, where the marquees were flattened to the ground. The Dales became a disaster area overnight. Many roads were totally blocked, farms cut off and terrible losses of both sheep and lambs were incurred. Hundreds of sheep died under drifts alongside stone walls where they had taken shelter and many were not found for weeks.

The early ground-nesting birds also suffered badly but the devotion of some of them was amazing. After the snow melted one of my shepherd friends came across a number of Golden Plovers sitting on eggs but frozen to death as they had gradually become covered.

On 2 May we decided to visit as many of our sites as possible to try to establish what

Mountain pansy in the middle valley

had happened to the Ouzels. At many of the regular sites there was no sign of them. We learned later that a number had been observed in gardens and even on bird tables in the neighbouring valleys. But at one bracken-covered site by a stream a male was seen on the bordering stone wall. He flew down, ran about 50 m and joined a female who was rooting about in a bracken clump. Over a period of one hour we watched her nest-building. She would make a 30 m flight to the stream, gather mud and return to the clump. From time to time she collected moss and small pieces of bracken from the area about 10 m from the nest. Each trip only took about two minutes and she seemed to be in a frantic hurry. She entered the clump from a different direction each time but always left by the same route. At no point did the male take any part in the nest-building although he was always in the vicinity. Hail was falling intermittently all afternoon.

On 4 May we visited the site and found a very lightly constructed nest about 30 cm above the ground in the bracken clump. It contained one cold egg and had no protection above whatever. The thaw had started on 27 April but it was unlikely that this nest

Too much hurry after the snow

could have been started before about 30 April — in which case the female built the complete nest and laid one egg in four days.

On 6 May the nest had one egg inside and one egg on the outside of the nest cup — this I placed inside. Three days later the female was sitting on four eggs and the male was singing on the wall about 40 m away. On 26 May the female came off the nest, which contained two young about six days old and two unhatched eggs.

On 30 May, which was a Saturday, there were a lot of people about and one couple walked past on each side of the nest. Both male and female were feeding the young when they had a chance to do so. By 4 June the young had flown, but two days later a fledgling was being fed by the male at the base of the wall about 75 m from the nest and although it was only about four days old it was flying quite strongly.

So this story did have a happy ending for one pair of Ouzels, although much wildlife perished as a result of the unseasonal blizzard.

The careless Ouzel

On 11 June '91 we found a second brood nest with one egg in a ravine about 300 m away from the successful first nest. This is the greatest distance separation we have recorded but the time gap between first brood leaving the nest and this first egg of the second one was a more normal nine days. On 12 June the female was sitting on two eggs and allowed me to touch the edge of the nest before coming off. On 14 June she came off, alarm-calling, when I was 30 m away and she still had two eggs.

On 16 June we returned to check the clutch. And again she came off the nest alarm-calling and flew down the ravine very close to the ground. About 30 m from the nest she flew straight into the side of a rock with an audible thump and fell fluttering and twitching to the ground. The male appeared from nearby and went to her, showing great agitation. She lay quite still on her back with legs in the air. We were quite sure she was dead. We climbed down the cliff but when we reached the spot both birds had disappeared!

We were certain that as a result of this accident the pair would desert. But two days later she was happily on the nest incubating her two eggs.

It would be nice if this story had a happy ending. But on 25 June when we visited to check if the young had hatched, we found only broken eggshells in and around the nest.

The shepherd

The Ouzel that trapped itself

On 15 May '89, having seen an Ouzel fly out, I was searching for a nest in a heather bank alongside a cart track. I was looking into the heather at eye level and my feet were in the bottom edge when I felt movement against my knee. Looking down I could vaguely see the outline of a nest containing two eggs and something struggling in the thick heather stems behind it. Further investigation revealed a female Ouzel which had obviously sat very tight and then found herself unable to come off the nest fowards because of my legs. In trying to escape backwards she had got herself hopelessly entangled.

With some difficulty and at the cost of a few feathers and much squawking, I was able to catch her. Held in the hand the lighter fringes to the feathers on her breast and underside were most striking, as was the pure yellow gape. Her gorget was very mixed brown and cream, giving the overall effect of a juvenile as there was no definite edge to the gorget. She was almost certainly a first-year bird. When released she flew off, alarm-calling and leaving a burst of small feathers behind. The male was nowhere to be seen or heard so that as a guard he was not very effective.

I was concerned that after being handled at the nest she might desert but two days later she was sitting. On 29 May the two eggs were actually hatching, giving a 14-day period of incubation at least. But on this occasion the male was in evidence when he attacked a Kestrel about 150 m from the nest and eventually chased it away.

The young were again observed on 7 June (nine days old), when they appeared fully feathered from above but still with a bare patch down the centre of the breast and under the wings.

The persistent Ouzel

At 09.30 on 3 May '91 I arrived at the Lower Crag and saw a female just below the top of the cliff. She flew quite silently to a lone rowan tree and there made her agitated *chook-chook* calls. She was then joined by the male, who took the top branch whilst she remained in the middle.

I returned down the valley and both birds followed me along the top edge of the crag, showing signs of agitation. They flew round in a large circle and returned. I retreated about 60 m to a sheltered corner. After about

First-year female Ouzel

eight minutes the female *chook-chooked* and in stages worked her way along the cliff face towards me — two or three times going into holes as if into a nest. Eventually she entered a large tuft of grass on the cliff face and stayed out of sight for about two minutes, *chook-chooking* continuously. She then flew back along the cliff and repeated the whole procedure. But this time she was quiet at the tuft of grass and remained there out of sight. After about ten minutes during which nothing happened, I approached and she flew off along the crag to the rowan tree, alarm-calling, and the male joined her there.

Behind the grass tuft I discovered a damaged nest which had been half pulled out with part of the lining and the front rim hanging outside the tuft. In the remainder was one warm egg, and there were no broken eggs inside or outside the nest. Had she returned to lay another egg — the nest having been predated only that morning? I decided to return later in the day.

At 16.15 the nest contained two cold eggs but there was no sign of the adults. So the female had indeed been desperate to lay a second egg, even though it meant sitting in a half-demolished nest to do it!

On 6 May I returned to check progress but found that the predator had returned, pulled out more of the nest and that broken pieces of shell lay on the ground below. The nest was about 2 m up the cliff so the predator was probably a Carrion Crow, of which there were a number in the vicinity.

The Ouzels that tricked us

On 21 June '86 we were crossing the moor in the Range Rover along a track which for part of the way ran between stone walls. As we approached a gateway leading onto the moor, we noticed a female Ouzel standing at the base of one of the stone pillars. As we approached she moved out into the track ahead of us and proceeded to flutter along about 20 m in front of the vehicle and only just above the ground. At one point she stopped and thinking she was injured I got out and tried to catch her. But she quickly resumed her unsteady progress, until after about 100 m she disappeared through a gate into a grassy field where she proceeded to feed quite normally.

It was only then that we realised that we had been deliberately misled and that she was engaging in a 'distraction display'. With hindsight we realised that when we first saw her,

there must have been one or more fledglings on the moor just through the gateway and she was deliberately leading us away from them.

A second instance was on 11 July '92 in the Escarpment territory. Here the track runs across the moor alongside a steeply rising heather and bilberry slope covered with enormous boulders. For nine years we have observed a pair of Ouzels in a 300 m section of this track and have spent countless hours watching them and searching in the hundreds of possible nesting places. We have heard the males singing at the beginning of the year, watched both adults feeding nearby and carrying the food to the rocks at the top — but then they disappear. Obviously they reach the nest totally undercover and although we have occasionally seen them fly out we have still not found the nest. Many years we have seen them feeding juveniles from both first and second broods. The problem is that we cannot get the Range Rover to a good observation point (O.P.) as the moor opposite the slope is very boggy and we cannot get off the track.

It is the only territory in which we have ever been defeated! But on 11 July on one of our last visits of the season we had an interesting experience there. It was 14.30 and raining so heavily that we had to keep the windscreen wipers on double speed in order to see anything. As we returned across the track a female Ouzel suddenly flew up from a tangle of small rocks and nettles right alongside the vehicle. She flew only 10 m and then landed. As we reached her she flew off again, very unsteadily, for another 10 m. This was followed by another flight of about 20 m and then she disappeared across the moor into the mist and falling rain.

Once again we realised that there must have been a very recently flown young one in the patch of nettles and we had just witnessed our second 'distraction display' by a Ring Ouzel.

This behaviour is common amongst many ground-nesting birds with nidifugous chicks (sometimes called 'downies') which can walk and leave the nest immediately they hatch. Earlier in the year we used to pass the nest of a Golden Plover alongside this same track. At first she always left the nest feigning injury by trailing a wing. But eventually she got so used to our Range Rover that she remained sitting even though the wheels passed within less than 1 m of the nest! We first found it with two eggs on 27 April and she still had only two on 2 May. By 6 May she was sitting on three eggs. By 15 May she actually allowed us to

Golden Plover

stop alongside and take photographs through the open window! My last personal observation was on 20 May, the day before I entered hospital for heart surgery. She was still sitting hard on three eggs.

Very fortunately one of my gamekeeper friends uses that track on most days going to or from the moor. At 04.30 on 1 June he actually saw one of the downies in the nest and the other two in the process of hatching. Depending exactly when she laid her third egg (sometime in the period 3–6 May), she had been incubating for between 26 and 29 days. It is incredible that this clutch survived for such a long period considering the great number of Carrion Crows and Gulls that we observed all through the period on that part of the moor.

But back to the Ring Ouzels and their 'distraction display'. Witherby reported a case in which the bird 'fluttered a few yards in a lazy sort of fashion'. Simms said distraction displays are recorded rarely and considered exceptional. So we have been very lucky to witness this type of behaviour on two separate occasions. Both times it seemed to have been induced by the vehicle — we have never seen it when observing Ouzels on foot.

Ouzels and Blackbirds

At the beginning of the season in March one frequently sees male Ouzels and Blackbirds in close company. They feed within a few feet of each other and move together as a pair. This might be expected at the treeline where their habitats overlap, but it often occurs well above the Blackbird's normal range in wilder parts of the moors where there is no tree cover. We have regularly seen them in the Bothy territory, which is 200 m above the treeline. But on 11 March '91 the Blackbird had a Fieldfare as companion and we did not see the first Ouzel for another three weeks.

Except at the treeline I have never observed a female of either species involved in this behaviour and the Blackbirds disappear from the higher territories when the female Ouzels start to arrive (see p. 60). At the treeline one has to be very careful about positively identifying a nest as that of an Ouzel or a Blackbird as the territories frequently overlap.

On 11 May '88 at an altitude of 280 m and just on the treeline we observed a male Ouzel and a male Blackbird about 80 m apart on electricity wires. They ignored each other but the Ouzel chased off another male Ouzel who attempted to enter the territory. In a derelict barn about 50 m away we located a very large and untidy nest constructed of reeds, bracken stems and bents which was exactly like an Ouzel's. It was empty. We returned on 28 May hoping to confirm that it was in fact an Ouzel's, but to our amazement found a female Blackbird sitting very tight on six eggs.

A male Ouzel was singing on the adjacent electricity wires and a pair were feeding in the field just over the wall. We eventually located three juvenile Ouzels flying around about 100 m from the barn, which to complicate matters still further also provided a home for a pair of Tawny Owls!

Another case of mistaken identity nearly occurred on 26 May '81. We observed a male Ouzel across a valley at maximum binocular range collecting food on a steep grassy slope just above the treeline. He flew six times into the edge of the trees in the valley bottom and disappeared — obviously feeding young. A thorough search revealed a typically untidy Ouzel-type nest of heather, bracken, reeds and bents about four feet above the ground in a small bushy tree. It contained four young about five–six days old. I returned four days later with camera equipment and hide hoping to get a photograph which would confirm that British Ouzels very occasionally do nest in trees. But to my chagrin the young, which at nine–ten days old were now well feathered, had a distinctly brownish hue and did not have the greyish feathers of the young Ouzel. Clearly this was a Blackbird's nest and although on that day the male Ouzel was singing from nearby we never found that nest.

A final example of a strange relationship between Ouzels and Blackbirds centres round a barn we discovered in '79. In that

The derelict barn at the treeline

year there was a Blackbird's nest with young on a beam inside and about 150 m away at the base of a rock on a steep bracken slope was an Ouzel, also with young. Ouzels have had a territory there every year since then and in most years Blackbirds have also been present. The barn is about 1 km beyond the treeline in a gently rising sheltered valley. For the last six consecutive years a pair of Little Owls have also nested there without predating either the Blackbirds or Ouzels.

But between the Blackbirds and Ouzels there is a lot of territorial aggression. Both like to sing from the chimney and also from an adjacent wall. We have never seen an actual fight but there has been a lot of wall top and flight chasing accompanied by angry calls from both parties.

On 20 May '88 I made the following notes whilst observing the barn area from the Range Rover parked on the opposite hillside and only about 100 m away.

17.15   A very agitated male Ouzel is making alarm calls on the wall in front of the barn. He flies across the valley, round in a circle behind me and lands on a wall about 150 m to the right, which forms his territory boundary and from which he frequently sings. A male Blackbird is standing quietly on a large boulder at the side of the barn.

17.28   Male Ouzel suddenly returns, making alarm calls, and he in alliance with female Blackbird proceeds to attack a Little Owl which has suddenly arrived. The Ouzel appears to hit the Owl, which crouches down in a hole on top of the wall.

17.33   Ouzel has attacked again and hit the Owl quite hard. Female Blackbird has disappeared. The Owl moves to another wall further away.

17.40   Male Blackbird is now singing on barn chimney, the Ouzel has disappeared and the Owl has moved to another wall.

Four days later we discovered the Ouzels' nest with four young in bracken about 80 m from the scene of the fight. They flew successfully, as did a second brood from a nest at about the same distance from the barn. It would appear that the Ouzel's and Blackbird's spirited attacks deterred the Little Owls from any attempt at predation.

In '58 D. W. Snow published his classic book *A Study of Blackbirds*, which concentrated on the Blackbird population of the

Blackbird (m)

Blackbird (f)

Botanic Garden at Oxford. It was reissued in '88 and a postscript was added mentioning a few of the more outstanding points on which new light had been thrown in the intervening years. It is a fascinating book recording in very great detail every facet of the Blackbird's behaviour. The comparison with the behaviour of the Ring Ouzel, which has come from my own observations, is of considerable interest. A few quotes of particular behaviour noted by Snow have been included in appropriate later chapters of this study.

Ouzels and neighbouring birds

On 21 March '90 whilst looking out for early Ouzels we were sitting in the Range Rover at Upper Crag (420 m). Within minutes a female Hen Harrier came hunting down the valley and then to our amazement we were treated to the unforgettable sight of a Peregrine Falcon landing on a grassy tuft on the cliff only 50 m from where we were sitting. With the naked eye we could see every detail of the speckled cream and black breast, the slate-blue back, the yellow legs, the fiercely hooked beak and the scimitar-shaped wings when it

eventually flew off. Within ten minutes it was back and was immediately joined by a second one. What a bonus after hours of fruitless Ouzel searching!

The year before on 29 May at this same crag we watched a pair of Ouzels feeding young in a nest behind a grass tuft about 7 m up the cliff face. 70 m nearer to us there was a Dipper sitting on five eggs, a Pied Wagtail on eggs and above them a Swallow building a nest on a ledge under an overhang — an amazing variety of birds at the same site.

In June '91 near a waterfall at an altitude of 250 m we found another group of nests all occupied at the same time. By a stretch of stream only 70 m long there was a Song Thrush sitting on three young, a Blackbird with three eggs, an Ouzel with five eggs and a Dipper sitting. A pair of Grey Wagtails were also present but we didn't locate the nest. This site was right on the treeline which usually separates the territories of Ouzels and Blackbirds.

But in the majority of its nesting sites the Ouzel is usually a loner with the occasional Wheatear or Meadow Pipit in the vicinity — and of course the ubiquitous Grouse.

Other upland birds

Merlin

A Schedule I bird and now very rare. The smallest British hawk, it hunts small birds, particularly Meadow Pipits, with great speed and accuracy. Once when we were watching a Wheatear at about 5 m from the Range Rover, a Merlin came over the bonnet and grabbed it in one foot. It then watched us quite calmly from a rock the same distance away for long enough for me to positively identify it from a bird book. Nests in heather.

Hen Harrier

A Schedule I bird and also very rare. Twice the size of a Merlin and hunts bigger prey, including the Ring Ouzel and small mammals. The female is brownish but the male has a most striking slate-grey head and upper parts with under parts pure white. Nests in heather.

Kestrel

The commonest bird of prey in Britain and the only one that can truly hover when locating its prey — predominantly voles, mice and occasionally small birds. Usually about four pairs nest in the valley in ruined buildings, old barns, cliffs and quarries. Ouzels are wary of them and attack them vigorously when they come near.

Kestrel (f)
with vole

Short-eared Owl

Truly diurnal, this large Owl can be seen quartering the moors at any time of the day as it searches mainly for small mammals. Nests amongst heather and lays five–eight eggs except in vole years, when it has been recorded with up to 13–14.

Red Grouse

Not found outside the British Isles. Able to survive on the moors throughout the winter. Protected from predators to provide moorland shooting after 12 August. The sanctuaries thus created help many of our rarest birds to survive, e.g. Hen Harrier, Merlin and even the Ring Ouzel itself. Nests among heather and lays six–ten eggs which are always at risk from Carrion Crows, foxes and stoats.

Meadow Pipit

The most plentiful bird of the uplands, it provides the staple diet for the avian hunters of the moors such as Merlin, Kestrel and Hen Harrier. Four–five brownish eggs are laid in a nest built of bents and well concealed in a hollow in the side of a tussock or in the edge of a moorland track.

Skylark

One of the songs that every country lover can recognise instantly as the bird climbs steadily upwards on a warm sunny day until it is out of sight. Unfortunately its numbers have been falling in recent years, probably due to modern farming methods disturbing its nesting habitat. Usually four brownish eggs in a well-hidden nest in the grass which can easily be confused with that of the Meadow Pipit.

Wheatear

Like the Ring Ouzel it winters in Africa and returns to the uplands at the same time. Nests in rabbit holes, under stones or in a wall. Lays five–six pale blue eggs. Its alarm call of *chak chak* is very similar to the Ouzel's but not as loud and dominating. Another call sounds as if two stones are being knocked together.

Golden Plover

Arrives early on the moors, when its peculiar alarm note carries for long distances. It

Short-eared Owl taken with 500 mm lens from the road

sounds like the opening of a rusty gate and can be written *tiu*. Nest is a small, scantily lined hollow in grass or peaty soil. Three–four eggs which take a long time to incubate — about four weeks. Recognised from direct flight and scimitar wings.

Lapwing

A common bird of the rough pastures of the uplands and on farms lower down. Normally four eggs in a rudimentary scrape, often on a slight mound to prevent becoming water-logged. Known by many different names from its familiar call of *peewit*, or as they say in the valley, *tewit*. Instantly recognised from its call and tumbling flight during the early breeding season.

Curlew

The nostalgic bubbling call of the curlew as it glides down over its territory in the breeding season epitomises for many the true spirit of the uplands. A large bird, it is instantly recognisable from the very long curved bill. It is able to open just the tip of this to extract food when digging in soft ground. Usually four eggs in nest well hidden in tussock but sometimes out in the open.

Curlew

Redshank

Seem to be increasing in numbers in the Dales where it is easily recognisable from its obviously waderlike appearance, brilliant red feet and legs and white wing flash when landing. Distinctive alarm call *tchee*. Nests in grassy tuft in marshy parts of the moor — well hidden and usually with four eggs.

Sandpiper

Nests alongside many Dales streams and rivers. Has a distinctive bobbing walk and a penetrating whistled cry when disturbed. Much smaller than the Redshank but similarly likes standing on fence posts and wall tops. A loner, not usually seen with others.

Oyster Catcher

Oyster Catcher

Usually a bird of the sea-shore, it has in recent years penetrated inland up the rivers. Sometimes called 'Sea-Pie' because of the distinctive black and white appearance. Most obvious features are straight orange-red bill, red eye and pink feet. Nests near water, often amidst shingle, with usually three eggs. Can now often be seen in the Dales and by our reservoirs.

Photographs of the other upland birds may be found elsewhere: Meadow Pipit, p. 39; Skylark, 39; Wheatear, 41; Red Grouse, 11; Golden Plover, 16; Lapwing, 48; Redshank, 49; Sandpiper, 49.

The Ring Ouzel study

General behaviour

When suddenly disturbed the Ring Ouzel seeks to escape by dashing downhill, taking advantage of every undulation and scrap of cover to make its escape. In seconds it disappears completely. But they are curious birds. Whilst one frantically searches the ground ahead, a glance behind will often reveal the bird on some prominent feature which it has reached by flying round in a large circle at quite a considerable height. Once it realises that you have spotted it the bird will often drop back into cover only to reappear a few seconds later 5–10 m away. This behaviour will be repeated over and over again and I have called the habit 'skyline peeping', as an Ouzel will always try to get above you to keep watch on your movements. They are clearly as anxious to keep track of the observer's position as he is of theirs.

When searching a territory we seek to get as high as possible ourselves and this is why a four-wheel drive vehicle is essential. Over the years we have worked out routes across coun try that bring us out above the various side valleys and alongside cliffs where we have always seen Ouzels in the past. With two of us in the vehicle these observation points (O.P.'s) enable us to keep watch all round for the first sign of movement.

The flight of the Ouzel is very distinctive. It is more dashing and direct than the Blackbird's and its wings appear to flicker — particularly as it travels away from one.

Trying to pick up a stationary Ouzel through binoculars can be very difficult. The dark plumage melts into the background and a white gorget can often be mistaken for a small piece of white limestone on the hillside — or vice versa. If they get suspicious when standing on a wall then without any previous movement they just 'drop off' on the blind side and disappear. Then the whole laborious process of locating them starts again.

The purpose of watching a male is the hope that he will go to the nest to visit the female who is sitting to check that all is well, or to let

Ouzel territory in the upper valley — four-wheel drive country

her come off for a short while to feed. The former can happen perhaps once per hour but the strain on one's eyes is considerable and so my wife and I take it in turns when thus employed.

If the bird observed is collecting food then of course the waiting period before it returns to the nest is likely to be very much less, except in one particular circumstance. If there are predators in the vicinity, Crows, Magpies or a Kestrel, then the wait can be interminable. In these circumstances we often move on and return later in the day if possible.

Many quite reputable bird books claim that the Ouzel has a very strong smell and can thus easily be found on its nest by dogs. Without doubt this is 'an old wives' tale' handed down from generation to generation. Certainly a good pointer can help to flush Ouzels off a nest in thick cover but no better than it can any form of game bird.

Choosing the right pair of binoculars is crucial. A cheap pair will ruin your eyes — they must be of a very high optical quality and that costs money. But they do not need to be of very high magnification so long as they have a really good field of view. 8 × 40 is an ideal combination which enables a flying Ouzel to be picked up quickly and followed. A telescope is useless for Ouzel spotting. The best combination of value for money, lightweight, rubber covering and good optics that I have found is the 8 × 40 Alpin Optolyth.

When returning to the nest an Ouzel will never fly directly to it. Individual birds vary in their degree of caution but quite often they will land 50 m or more away. They then work their way to the nest on the ground a few metres at a time, taking advantage of any cover available. They usually develop a standard approach route but the male and female usually have different ones. Leaving the nest is the Achilles' heel of the Ouzel species. They usually fly straight out without taking any precautions to confuse an observer. The golden rule therefore is that a nest is not where a flying Ouzel lands but from where it takes off.

Were it not for this weakness it would be virtually impossible to find a nest on a bracken or heather covered hillside, however good a view one had of it. The bird on landing just disappears under the cover and it is then best to wait for it to fly out, using the naked eye in order to widen the field of vision. It is often wise to remain concealed through two or three visits before actually trying to find the nest, particularly if it is under overhanging heather.

Shakehole: not just a second brood — but a third brood also

On Easter Monday '91 I was walking towards a shakehole in one of our highest territories at 450 m. There was a howling wind, heavy rain and thick mist. It was my seventh visit in two weeks and already the date, 1 April, was the latest I had reached in seven years without seeing the first Ouzel in the valley. Then suddenly I saw it. A brownish-black shadow flew from the far edge of the shakehole, crossed the stream and disappeared into the mist on the moor beyond — an Ouzel, certainly, but impossible to say whether it was male or female. And so began the most remarkable year's history of any pair of Ouzels we have ever observed.

The following day, 2 April, was also wet and windy but with better visibility. My wife and I both had an excellent view through binoculars as a male and female came up from the bottom of the shakehole and flew off over the moor. They were below us and their wing flashes were very obvious.

A pair of Ouzels had nested in this shakehole for the previous four years — usually building nests on the same rocky ledge behind hanging heather. The remains of two of these old nests were still there — just sodden heaps of moss and bents. But four days later on 6 April the left-hand one of these had been transformed into a brand-new nest complete with a deep cup lined with fine dry

Shakehole nest with 'tell-tale'

grasses. By 8 April a 20 cm piece of dead bracken stem had been woven into the rim and was hanging down in typical Ouzel 'telltale' fashion. On the 13th the nest contained one cold egg — the earliest egg by five days we have ever recorded, notwithstanding the late arrival of the adults. From arrival at the shakehole to producing the first egg in a newly constructed nest in 12 days is a remarkable achievement.

The timetable went to plan with one egg per day until the clutch of four was completed on 16 April. But when we visited the site on 23 April, both adults were very agitated and complaining loudly. We found that three eggs had disappeared from the nest and only one remained. Some large pieces of eggshell were lying about 15 m away. The predator was almost certainly a stoat, probably living in the jumble of boulders at the bottom of the shakehole. We were very downcast at losing this nest so early in the season, particularly as we had a perfect history of the site, with two successful broods in each of the previous three years.

But all was not lost! A week later, the male was seen about 200 m upstream and on 3 May the male and female were in the same area alarm-calling. On 18 May we found a nest about 250 m upstream from the shakehole containing four eggs. It was on a ledge under a bank and shielded by overhanging heather.

So here was a proven replacement (second) brood and I was later able to calculate from the age of the young that the first egg must have been laid on 11 May. Judging from the distress of the adults the first nest was predated on or just before 23 April, so it had taken them about 18 days to locate a new site in the territory, build a new nest and produce the first egg. Compared with other territories we had studied this was a long interval. Five–six days appears to be the mean gap between broods, but at the end of April there was a very bad spell of cold and windy weather at the Shakehole territory, which may have delayed the re-nesting.

The second brood young flew successfully on 10 June. On 12 June the male and female were alarm-calling back at the shakehole and the flown young were only 50 m away, having moved about 200 m downstream from the second brood nest.

In the shakehole itself I found to my amazement a third nest had been built on top of the debris of the 1990 first brood nest and only about 3 m from the 1991 first nest. It was complete except for the lining but some new lining had been added to the predated 1991

nest, from which the single remaining egg had disappeared!

Two days later, on 14 June, the third '91 nest was unchanged (still unlined), but the first predated '91 nest had been completely refurbished and was fully lined. Visits on 16 and 22 June showed no change in the situation but there was very heavy rain in the period.

Although it was very late in the season, I decided on 6 July once again to check the situation in the Shakehole territory. As we arrived at the stream above the shakehole a female was feeding and she flew upstream. I followed and about 80 m above the site of the successful replacement (second) brood nest she came out from the heather on the opposite bank from a very neat nest containing three eggs. Later we were able to calculate that the first egg of this third brood (but fourth nest) was laid on 23 June, just 13 days after the second brood left the nest, but during this period she had of course built another nest (the third) back at the shakehole and renovated her first nest! The three young hatched on 9 July and left the nest on 21 July exactly 12 days later.

And so ended successfully the '91 saga of this tenacious pair of Ouzels, who in one season:

— were the first pair to arrive in the valley on 1 April;
— built a nest and laid their first egg in 12 days on 13 April;
— had that nest predated on or just before 23 April;
— built a second nest and laid the first egg in it on 11 May;
— successfully reared these young, which flew on 10 June;
— built a third nest and relined the first nest;
— built a fourth nest and laid the first egg on 23 June;
— successfully reared this third brood, which flew on 21 July.

Shakehole was not a fluke

The adjacent territory to Shakehole is Upper Crag, whose centre is 550 m across the moor and similarly has a stream running through it. The difference is that whereas the Shakehole territory is all wild moorland and heather banks, Upper Crag consists mainly of a cliff 20 m high and 200 m long with rocky ledges and crevices. Nearby are steep grassy slopes cropped close by the sheep and which provide an ideal feeding ground.

On 6 April '91 a male Ouzel was feeding in this area and on 10 and 15 April male and

TABLE 1. MULTIPLE BROODS AT SHAKEHOLE AND UPPER CRAG TERRITORIES

| | Shakehole | | | | | Upper Crag |
	1988	1989	1990	1991	1992	1991
First Ouzel seen in the valley	22 Mar	25 Mar	16 Mar	1 Apr	31 Mar	1 Apr
First Ouzel seen in this territory	4 Apr	17 Apr	16 Mar	1 Apr	10 Apr	6 Apr
Site of nest	3 m from '87 nest	Same as '88	Same as '88/'89	Same as '87	Same as '88/'89/'90	10 m from '88/'89/'90 2nd brood nest
1st Brood Date of 1st egg	19 Apr	21 Apr	30 Apr	13 Apr	26 Apr	27 Apr
Number of eggs	4	3	4	4	4	4
Incubation period in days	14	14	14	—	13	—
Date of hatching	6 May	7 May	17 May	Predated about 23 Apr	12 May	Predated on 12 May
Nestling period in days	—	14	—	—	13	—
Young left nest	20 May(E)	21 May	30 May(E)	—	25 May	—
2nd Brood Gap between broods in days	8(E)	9	11(E)	18(E)	8(E)	7(E)
Site of nest	Same as 1st brood	Same as 1st brood	15 m from 1st brood	250 m from 1st brood	60 m from 1st brood	60 m from 1st brood
Date of 1st egg	28 May(E)	30 May	10 Jun(E)	11 May(E)	2 Jun(E)	19 May(E)
Number of eggs	4	4	4	4	5	3
Incubation period in days	—	—	—	—	—	—
Date of hatching	14 Jun	15 Jun	27 Jun(E)	28 May	20 Jun	4 Jun(E)
Nestling period in days	—	—	—	13	—	—
Young left nest	28 Jun(E)	29 Jun(E)	11 Jul(E)	10 Jun	Predated	18 Jun
3rd Brood Gap between broods in days	—	—	—	13(E)	—	5
Site of nest	—	—	—	80 m from 2nd brood	—	Same as 1st brood
Date of 1st egg	—	—	—	23 Jun(E)	—	23 Jun
Number of eggs	—	—	—	3	—	4
Incubation period in days	—	—	—	—	—	—
Date of hatching	—	—	—	9 Jul	—	8 Jul
Nestling period in days	—	—	—	12	—	12
Young left nest	—	—	—	21 Jul	—	20 Jul

Estimated dates (E) assume 14-day periods for incubation and as nestlings.
At Shakehole in 1991 another nest was built between the 2nd and 3rd broods but not laid in.

c

First nest at Upper Crag — also used for third clutch

female were both present. On 26 April we found a nest ready for eggs about 3 m up the cliff on a grassy ledge. On 30 April the female was sitting on four eggs, which meant she had laid her first egg on 27 April.

On 11 May the female was sitting but by 13 May all the eggs had disappeared. The nest was undamaged and as the intervening day was Sunday, and there had been a number of hikers about, this may have been a case of human predation. On 22 May the female came off a nest about 60 m away and about 5 m up the cliff in a rocky cleft. It was inaccessible but through binoculars we could see the nest from the rising moorland opposite.

On 11 June it was raining heavily and the female was sitting high on the nest, obviously shielding young. On 18 June we watched at least three of these being fed by both male and female amongst the boulders at the foot of the cliff, and from their size, plumage and behaviour they had almost certainly left the nest that morning. If so one can calculate that the first egg (of this second nest) was laid on or about 19 May, which means that this pair built a new nest and laid the first egg within seven days of losing their first clutch!

On 22 June, just four days after the second brood left the nest, we observed, at a distance of only 15 m from the Range Rover, the male and female copulate three times. Each act of copulation took about five seconds with a ten-second break between. The female was carrying a beakful of dried bents all the time with the stems arranged sideways and so was presumably in the process of lining a third nest!

On 25 June the female flew off the first brood nest, which had been renovated and contained three eggs. This meant that the first egg was probably laid on 23 June, the day after we saw the male and female copulating

only about 10 m away from the nest. As the second brood left the nest on 18 June there was thus a gap of only five days before the female was sitting on the first egg of the third brood in a nest which had previously been used for the first brood and then predated!

The third clutch, by then four eggs, hatched on 8 July, giving an incubation period of 12 days. The four young flew successfully from the nest on 20 July, just 12 days after hatching and one day before the third brood young in the adjacent territory at Shakehole.

This Upper Crag territory also had a very successful history of two broods in each of the three years, '88/'89/'90. In each year the first nest was in an inaccessible cleft about 15 m up the cliff at the left-hand end and the second nest was in a similar position at the right-hand end about 200 m away. The implication is that in those three years they were the same adults, or certainly the same female, but that in '91 they were not, as the nesting sites were different. In '92 two broods were again produced but in two new sites on the cliff face. But what *is* certain is that Shakehole and Upper Crag have been our two most successful territories for five consecutive years.

They are at the highest altitude (450 m), only 550 m apart and in '91 each pair laid three clutches and successfully reared two of them. Over the five-year period '88–'92 they produced 22 clutches between them, which would seem to indicate pretty conclusively that Ring Ouzels do have two broods much more frequently than has hitherto been thought. This subject is more fully discussed in a later chapter.

Dusky Maiden

On 25 March '89 we saw our first male Ouzel in the lower valley and five more appeared in the next few days, together with a lot of Wheatears. A male Ouzel returned to the Bothy territory at 450 m on 30 March, and on 1 April we had lunch in the Range Rover at the bottom of the narrow boulder-strewn gulley leading up to the nearby shakehole. After about 45 minutes' observation a pair of Ouzels appeared only 20 m from us. He was feeding normally but she was clearly ravenous and devoured a large number of worms which she tugged out of the damp grass and peat. After 15 minutes she flew into the lee of a nearby wall and rested. She was the first female we had seen that year and had probably just arrived.

She was a very brown bird with a dusky gorget, whitish wing patches and a beautifully marked breast — almost certainly a first-year bird. He also had good wing patches, clearly fringed feathers on the breast and a gorget which was heavily marked with black. It was not clearcut and was not white all over

and again we thought he was probably in his first year.

She was a truly beautiful bird and we immediately christened her Dusky Maiden. We visited the territory six more times and watched the pair on each occasion. Eventually on 9 May we located the nest containing

Dusky Maiden

Dusky Maiden's mate

three eggs, very well concealed in a rabbit scrape under a stone in a heather slope about 75 m from our O.P. We were later able to calculate that the first egg had been laid about 24 April. The nest was very neat and made of dead heather stems lined with bents. She had made an apron of freshly picked heather flowers in front of the nest. Many Ouzels indulge in some form of nest decoration or tell-tale in this way.

22 May was a perfect sunny day with no wind. I arrived to set up my hide at 08.15 on the opposite side of the gulley and at a range of 13 m. The male was nowhere to be seen but Dusky Maiden immediately got very angry and came on to rocks only 10 m away from me, alarm-calling *chak-chak* the whole time. When I went to the nest itself to check the young, she attacked me like a Mistle Thrush. She repeatedly came straight at me and forced me to duck.

I entered the hide at 09.00 but 15 minutes later one of the young, which was strengthening its wings by flapping on the edge of the nest, overbalanced. It tumbled about 7 m down the slope. There was nothing for it but to emerge from the hide and put it back in the nest to the accompaniment of much screeching. This disturbed the other two, who scrambled out of the nest and into the back of the hole it.

Within five minutes Dusky Maiden returned to the area round the nest but she did not bring food. However, she did remove some faecal sacs which the young had dropped in and near the nest. Presumably this was to avoid them being seen by predators.

At 12.00 the male appeared with food and went very quickly to the nest and fed the young in turn. Shortly afterwards she also arrived with food and they fed the young alternately about every 15 minutes until I left about 01.30, having used up all my film — five rolls of 36 exposures each!

On 24 May we watched both adults feeding the fledglings in the heather along the gulley, so presumably they left the nest on 23 May. On 29 May we saw nothing but on 6 June the male fed and 'slept' in the gulley for about an hour. Then Dusky Maiden came from behind us, flew up the gulley and disappeared into the shakehole beyond. I found her sitting on two eggs in a nest precisely where we had found second brood nests in '87 and '88. On 12 June she still had two eggs, and was very aggressive and once again attacked me. On 14 June at 15.30 she had one egg and one tiny young and on 20 June she had two young

which by then were exactly six days old. Once again she was very aggressive but he did not appear at all.

The gap between the young of the first brood leaving the nest on 23 May and the first egg of the second brood being laid can be calculated as seven days, during which she was helping to feed the first brood and also building the second nest.

We both looked forward to renewing acquaintance with Dusky Maiden in '90. A male Ouzel returned to Bothy on 18 March and she was there by 6 April, maybe sooner, as our visit was delayed. We found her nest on 1 May with four eggs only a few metres from the '89 first brood site. On 9 May it contained four young about two days old. This indicated that the first egg was laid about 20 April.

I returned on 15 May and took three hours of video film in two sessions at the nest. Dusky Maiden was as unafraid as ever and came to within 7 m of me to have her pictures taken out in the open using my ordinary camera, hand-held with a 500 mm lens.

On 19 May we returned but the gulley was quiet and there were no birds about. With a sense of foreboding I approached the nest. The worst had happened. Only a few small feathers, a head and a leg remained of the

All that was left of Dusky Maiden's family

four young but worse still were the wing and tail feathers of an adult.

Dusky Maiden was dead. Perhaps her aggression had been her downfall. Perhaps she had attacked the predator, probably a stoat, instead of abandoning her family and saving herself. Nature can be very cruel and these tragedies are hard for a human to accept. We both miss her — she was our favourite Ouzel.

Nests and locations

In Britain Ouzels nest at or above the treeline. They do not venture into woods or fir plantations, preferring the open spaces of the wilder moorland and rocky upland valleys. In this they differ completely from the Blackbird, which is a more skulking bird that slips into the nearest cover when threatened.

In their study of 297 BTO nest record cards from all over Britain, Flegg and Glue found that 82 per cent of the nests reported lay between 230 and 530 m. The lowest was in Sutherland at 30 m where the treeline is virtually at sea level. Many bird books use expressions like 'usually found above 250 m' (before metrication the magic height was 1,000 ft), as if the birds carried an altimeter to determine their nesting habitat. Not one book refers to the treeline as being the critical factor. In the Pennines the treeline is about 250 m and it is at this height we found our lowest nest in the study area.

So do Ouzels ever nest in trees? There are often isolated rowans, hawthorns or birches in sheltered places above the treeline but in 15 years and 164 occupied nests we have never found one in a tree — except the roots of ones growing on cliffs. Flegg and Glue had five cases in 297 nests so that out of the grand total of our nests and theirs — 461 — only 1.1 per cent were in trees. Yet the Reader's Digest *Guide to the Birds of Britain* says, 'The Ring Ouzel nests in a tree if one is available . . .', and shows a female Ouzel feeding young in a nest in a tree. Just how misleading can a popular publication be? Strangely the Alpine Ring Ouzel *does* nest mainly in trees as do Fieldfares, with whom they often share their nesting habitat.

The terrain of the detailed study area is described in an earlier chapter but the locations of individual nests within it are analysed in Table 2. The groupings are those used by Flegg and Glue so that a direct comparison can be made with their research. The most significant figures are for those locations marked with an asterisk (*). These are mainly man-made and are places that would be visited by ornithologists looking for nests in general. An Ouzel's nest in any of them would be fairly obvious. Flegg and Glue's total of 39 per cent compares with only 16 per cent for ourselves. I think this can be attri-

TABLE 2.   NESTING LOCATION

Location	Flegg and Glue		Appleyard	
	No.	Per cent	No.	Per cent
Crag or cliff	29	12	37	23
Gully or gorge	54	21	48	29
Grass or heather slopes	70	28	52	32
Quarry*	24	10	9	5
Wall or building*	34	14	9	5
Pothole or shaft*	20	8	3	2
Track or cutting*	18	7	6	4
TOTAL	249	100	164	100

* Mainly man-made

buted to the fact that we have thoroughly searched everywhere in the detailed study area over many years — not just in the obvious places.

Our figures show that a total of 84 per cent of the nests are in the more remote, difficult to search and inaccessible situations. In my view they give a more accurate guide to the actual distribution of nests in a given area. One common factor amongst the 84 per cent of nests is that they are usually close to some prominent feature in the general habitat, e.g. a lone tree, a rocky outcrop or a gulley. These often occur by a stream which also provides the softer ground where the Ouzels can obtain food with the minimum amount of flying. Thus the middle of an open, flat moor is not the place to look for nests and I have never found one in such a situation. Nor did Durman.

The steps in nest-finding start when the male birds start singing — usually the first week in April in the study area. The first song is not necessarily heard at the lowest altitude but can be in any of the territories from 250–500 m. But the nest will most usually be found within 25 m of the principal singing place — be it tree, crag, ruined building or wall. At the start of the season there is no alternative to a cold search of all the likely places and particularly those favoured in previous years.

One may be assisted by seeing the pair prospecting for a nesting site. The male, who has arrived in the territory before the female, can sometimes be seen showing her suitable places which she carefully inspects before moving on to his next suggestion. Once the site has been selected, the nest is built entirely by the female whilst the male stands guard on a prominent feature nearby and often sings.

Durman agrees that the male does not help to build the nest.

This is constructed of reeds, heather, dead bracken and strong grasses with a mud strengthening in the base and is lined with bents. It can vary from a very untidy large structure standing clear of its surroundings on a ledge, to a neat cup of moss completely sunk into the grass or peat. Often the nest is

Nest sunken into grassy ledge

adorned with small sprigs of heather and moss and frequently a large 'tell-tale' may be added, such as a 20 cm length of dead bracken or wool left to blow about in the wind. A site is usually chosen with overhead cover — under a rock on a slope, on a ledge under an overhang, in a hole in a wall or building, and under or in heather or bracken. Early in the season these latter nests can be very obvious when viewed from above and are very prone to predation by Crows or Magpies.

Nest-building

At 12.20 on 11 June '83 we arrived at an O.P. overlooking the Barn territory. We could hear a male singing and eventually located him on a skyline wall behind us. The female appeared occasionally and appeared to be feeding young. After an hour we climbed up and disturbed both adults with four juveniles which we judged had left the nest between one and two weeks previously. They had tails of about 5 cm, could fly strongly, had light-coloured wing flashes and spotted breasts and were still a little fluffy about the head.

We had first seen the male near the Barn on 5 April, and on our next visit on 30 April a female was with him and he was singing from a wall. Later he was chasing her on the ground in the valley bottom near the stream. In my diary for that day I speculated that they might be about to mate. As this often occurs very near the date of the first egg this was probably laid on about 1 May, which would make the juveniles about 11 days out of the nest (which we never found) on the day we saw them.

At 14.00 on 11 June both adults appeared on the ground within 30 m of the Range Rover, and about 14.15 both of them kept disappearing under a small rock carrying building materials. After five minutes he wearied of this 'manual' labour and went about 10 m up the slope where he went on guard. Meanwhile the female was obviously building a nest in a crack behind a climbing plant on the cliff near by.

The timetable then went as follows:

14.20   Female visits nest and departs. Male on guard above.
14.23   Female returns with beakful of nest material and departs.
14.25   Female returns with more material and departs. Male now singing in tree about 20 m away.
14.27   Female returns with beakful and leaves after 15 seconds.
14.29   Female returns with more material and stays five minutes, during which she is moving all over the nest. She then flies off up the gorge and disappears.

At 14.50 I left the Range Rover and went to the nest in the rock face. It was virtually completed. We were later able to calculate that the first egg of this second brood was laid on about 12 June (the next day).

I also looked under the stone in which both male and female had shown an interest. There were only about four beakfuls of nesting material there. Presumably they had been enacting some kind of courtship ritual, but at no time did he take any part in building the actual nest.

On 13 May '91 it rained all morning but the sun broke through about 12.30. We were sitting in the Range Rover in the Bothy territory at the bottom of a steeply rising valley with a grassy bottom and steep heather slopes and boulders on each side. A male began to sing from a rock about 100 m from us at the edge of the heather. We then located the female foraging about in the grass below him. She had a large pinkish-white gorget and strong wing markings. She was probably about three years old.

She hopped up the slope into the heather where she eventually disappeared into a heather clump. Two minutes later she flew straight out and into the grass about 20 m below. She foraged there for ten minutes then flew directly back to the heather clump and went into it. She repeated this excursion to the grass three more times and appeared to be carrying grass held crossways in her beak on the return trip. On one occasion she was chased by the male all the way to the clump. They kept landing, chasing on the ground and taking off again. On arrival the male tried to copulate with her three times by jumping on her back but she evaded him and went into the clump. He stood about 0.5 m away and watched her closely. After two minutes she emerged, and flew back to the grass whilst he returned to his rock and sang a few piping notes. The action went on for about an hour, at which time I decided to investigate.

Behind the heather clump was a nearly finished nest with bents being woven into the lining. Some decoration had been added to the outside, consisting of heather twigs and burnt heather pieces at the front base of the nest. An examination of the grass to which she had returned each time was most illuminating. She had dragged beakfuls out of it and

years and had suggested this site to his new mate, as there were dozens of other suitable ones in the territory. What is quite certain is that he took no part in the actual building of the nest itself.

The first egg was laid on 15 May just two days after the nest-building described. She laid five in total, which hatched successfully but were predated on 11 June, probably by a stoat. But unlike Dusky Maiden this female escaped and built a second nest in a shakehole about 70 m away. Once again she produced a clutch of five, the first of which was laid on 19 June just eight days after the predation of the first brood.

But once again tragedy struck the Bothy territory. Just two days before the young should have left the nest a party of potholers began digging nearby and the adults could not get to the nest. It was raining, cold and windy and all the nestlings died of exposure and starvation.

Eggs and length of season

The eggs are similar to those of a Blackbird but with a green hue to the blue. They are similarly marked with small blotches of reddish

Collecting area for nesting materials

Typical nest and eggs in bracken

an area of about 5 × 2 m was very obviously disturbed.

In '89 and '90 Dusky Maiden (see an earlier chapter) had nested in this same territory. The '91 nest was only 10 m from where she had built, but Dusky Maiden had been killed. So perhaps the male was from the previous

brown but these are more distinct and separated than with the Blackbird.

The usual clutch is three–five. An analysis of 85 clutches in the ten seasons '82–'91 produced an overall mean of 3.93 eggs compared with Flegg and Glue's overall mean of 4.1 eggs from 79 clutches, and Durman's 4.05

Freak egg probably laid by a first-year bird

eggs from 19 clutches. From all three sources there were 735 eggs from 183 clutches which produced an overall mean of 4.0 eggs per clutch. If my own figures are split between first-brood clutches and second/third-brood clutches, then the means become 3.98 and 3.76. This seems to indicate that clutches later in the season are slightly smaller, perhaps due to the poorer availability of food.

So far as brood size (i.e., young successfully reared) is concerned, my figures show a mean of 3.6 young per nest, which exactly accords with the figure produced by Flegg and Glue.

Sometimes one is lucky enough to find a nest before laying starts (as was the case at Shakehole in 1991). By visiting it every day one can then determine an exact first egg date and the dates for subsequent eggs in the clutch. But more often the nest is found after incubation has commenced and then the date of hatching or the estimated age of the young has to be used to calculate the date of the first egg. For this purpose an assumption has to be made on the length of the average incubation period. This has been taken as 14 days to accord with the figure used by Flegg and Glue (but see later for the actual length of incubation).

Two histograms are shown giving first egg dates of 93 clutches in the 13 seasons '79–'91 and 53 clutches in the four seasons '88–'91. The first one includes every nest I have ever found in the valley in which it was possible to establish a first egg date. But in the early days I did not realise how many Ouzels had two broods and used to stop my research in mid-June. The second histogram covers just four seasons of more intensive study when I was able to spend more time in the field due to retirement. It is therefore more representative of the pattern of clutches in one particular area over the breeding season as a whole. The horizontal scale covers five-day periods.

It will be seen that there is a very clear initial peak of laying in the last ten days of April. The earliest egg we have ever recorded was on 13 April '91 and this was an actual date, not an estimated one. The mean date over 13 seasons is 22 April. It is interesting that the earliest observed male Ouzel in the valley was on 15 March and the mean over six seasons has been 25 March. This gives a mean interval of four weeks from date of arrival of the males for them to establish a territory, find a mate and for her to build a nest and lay the first egg.

In the histograms there is a second very distinct peak in the five-day period from 11–15 May. This can only be explained by the incidence of replacement clutches for those predated in or after the initial period of laying. The third peak occurs from 26 May–4 June and is definitely comprised of normal second clutches, which are a lot more common than has previously been supposed. The earliest first egg of a second brood was 26 May.

A surprising number of first eggs occur in the 15-day period from 10–24 June. Some of these may be second clutches from late nesting pairs but the period contains two proven cases of third clutches after replacement clutches and some of the others may well fall into this category also. What is quite certain is that in a favourable year the season can extend much later than has hitherto been appreciated.

Flegg and Glue have this to say: 'There is a clear peak of laying at the end of April and in early May. While a small proportion of nests were recorded as "second broods", there is only a relatively slight indication of a secondary peak in late May and early June, suggesting that many fewer pairs are double brooded than Witherby and Bannerman imply. The situation is obscured by late-laying birds and replacement clutches.' There is no doubt that their conclusion on the frequency of second broods is wrong and caused by the fact that the observers completing the Nest Record Cards were not Ring Ouzel specialists.

TABLE 3. FIRST EGG DATES (in 5-day periods)

	Apr 11–15	Apr 16–20	Apr 21–25	Apr 26–30	May 1–5	May 6–10	May 11–15	May 16–20	May 21–25	May 26–30	M–Ju 31–4	Jun 5–9	Jun 10–14	Jun 15–19	Jun 20–24		Tot.
1979–91	1	9	14	15	4	3	8	5	4	12	7	3	3	3	2		93
1988–91	1	3	9	8	1	1	6	2	2	9	4	0	2	3	2		53

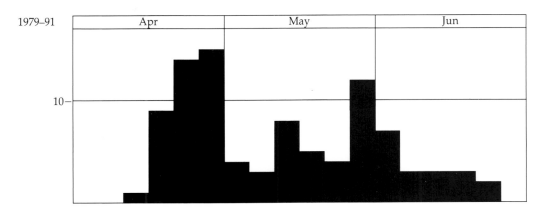

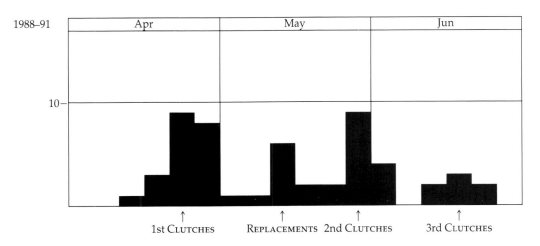

1st CLUTCHES   REPLACEMENTS   2nd CLUTCHES   3rd CLUTCHES

Incubation and nestling periods

Virtually no reliable data has been published on these subjects because of the difficulty of getting a firm date for the laying of the last egg and firm dates for the actual hatching and for leaving the nest. Flegg and Glue quoted only two cases of incubation periods which they could calculate from the BTO Nest Record Cards. These produced periods of 12 days and eight days. They comment, 'The second must remain suspect until further data are available. Witherby et al. (1938) and Banner-man (1954) both give 14 days without sample sizes or references.' BWP gives 12–14 days, again without references. Simms gives 12–14 days from his own observations in the Pennines in the 1940s.

I have been able to establish the period precisely in ten different cases — five of 12 days, two of 13 days and three of 14 days. These produce a mean period of 12.8 days. BWP's and Simms' 12–14 days therefore appear to be correct and cover variations brought about by different weather conditions.

The nestling becomes a fledgling in 12–14 days

Nestlings hatching with discarded eggshell behind nest

So far as the nestling period is concerned, there is once again a wide diversity of opinion amongst the experts. Flegg and Glue quote periods of 10, 12, 13 and 16 days. Witherby and Bannerman both elect for 14 days without references. BWP quotes 14–16 days, Poxton says 13–15 days and Simms quotes from his own observations 12, 13, 13 and 14.

In five specific cases I recorded three periods of 12 days, one of 13 days and one of 14. Much depends on the degree to which a nest is subject to disturbance. Once the young become agitated they tend to leave the nest earlier. I would give the normal spread of days as 12–14.

My own observations indicate that incubation is undertaken by the female only, except for short periods when she is off the nest feeding. Particularly in cold, windy or wet weather the male will protect the eggs but gives way to the female as soon as she has fed. I believe that many observers who are unused to the Ring Ouzel as a species record the bird coming off the nest as female if it has a muddy-coloured gorget, but as male if it appears to have a white one. As has been pointed out earlier, second year and older females can be similar to a male and great care must therefore be taken in identification in these circumstances.

So far as feeding the young is concerned, there are no differences of opinion. Both adults feed the young but I have noted that the female always seems to work harder. The male will often leave her to carry on whilst he stands guard nearby. This whole subject of behaviour at the nest is dealt with in a later chapter, as also is the controversial one of the degree to which Ring Ouzels are double-brooded.

Behaviour at the nest

In the 11 seasons '80–'90 I set up my hide at 19 different Ring Ouzel nests for periods which usually lasted between four and five hours. As a result I had a collection of some thousands of colour photographs and slides from which to choose the illustrations for this book. They speak for themselves and illustrate Ouzel behaviour at and around the nest better than any description I could give.

When the young are hatching or very tiny a female will sit so tight that she actually has to be touched before she will come off the nest. When she comes off voluntarily to feed, the male will shelter very small young from rain, wind or hot sunshine but I have never seen one actually on a nest for more than a period of about ten minutes. This is long enough for the female to get some food for herself and to bring some back for small young. Once the young have some feathers on their backs, at about five days, they can be left for longer periods whilst both parents fetch food. But the female often seems to do more of this work than he does.

As a parent returns to the nest the young hear it arriving and crane their heads upward with yellow gapes wide open. Depending on the amount brought, two or three young are fed and then the parent touches the rear of one of them with its beak. It up-ends and excretes a white faecal sac, which is usually swallowed by the parent at once before repeating the procedure. Up to three sacs are swallowed or sometimes two with a third being carried away for disposal. Virtually every time food is brought to the nest, one or more sacs are taken.

Anticipation

Excretion of faecal sac

The regularity of feeding varies greatly throughout the day, with the busiest time being the morning. Around noon there is often a break of up to an hour or more. All activity is suspended if there are predators, usually Crows, in the vicinity or flying overhead.

I have carefully analysed the feeding pattern at two very different nesting sites. At Watersplash on 26 May '83 the nest was in a bank of bilberry about 20 m from a stream with excellent damp feeding areas on both sides for about 200 m. There had been heavy rain for much of the previous two weeks. At Ravine on 16 July '83 the nest was behind ferns on a low cliff with a large grass field containing sheep about 100 m away. The weather had been dry and very warm for the previous three weeks. The young at both nests were about ten days old. At Watersplash the female averaged 22 minutes between visits and the male 15 minutes. At Ravine the female averaged 27 minutes and the male 22 minutes. At both nests the male appeared to bring less food per visit than the female. He probably stayed nearer the nest to keep watch for predators and did not fly to the more distant optimum feeding area.

There is no doubt that the Watersplash parents feeding a first brood (26 May) had a lot easier time collecting food in the damp surroundings than did those with a second brood at Ravine where it was bone dry (16 July). This is reflected in the greater time that it took them to collect food between visits.

Normally the parents are never at the nest at the same time but seem to arrange their visits so that the nestlings do not have to wait too long between feeds. This means that usually they are being fed by one or other parent about every 10–15 minutes. But the male

Ouzel (m) on guard

First-year female approaching nest

Her mate with a good beakful of food

often takes quite long periods off during which he stands guard nearby. Often this is after he returns to the nest area from collecting food and the prey can be seen wriggling about in his beak the whole time. He appears to go into a kind of trance and remains quite stationary with his head sunk between his shoulders. I call it 'going to sleep' although he never closes his eyes.

I first photographed Ouzels in the Watersplash territory on 4 June '80 and my diary records some interesting observations made that day. Because I had not yet got a 1000 mm lens I was using the original 500 mm and set up the hide at 10.30 at a range of only 6 m, which is very close. The young were about eight days old. Both adults came back quite quickly but it took her about an hour to get to the nest with food. She was a beautifully marked first-year bird, with a very muddy gorget. She fed the young only three times in 2.5 hours. He stayed on guard for about 15 minutes at a time with no movement at all, often only 3–4 m from the nest. His beak was full of live worms, caterpillars and moths. She eventually came with food about every 20–30 minutes. It took the male until 15.10 (nearly five hours) to pluck up courage and actually feed the young.

Another long day in the hide was on 30 May '84 in the territory we call Richard's Top, which is very isolated. I entered the hide 14 m from the nest at 07.45 in thick mist. The male returned very quickly and fed the young at 08.05 and at 08.25, but I couldn't photograph him as the droplets of mist were condensing on my lens. By 08.55 the sun had dried the camera and he fed the young and again at 09.06 and 09.35. So he made five

visits in 90 minutes — an average of one visit every 18 minutes.

The female was much more cautious and did not approach the nest until 10.10 — 2.5 hours after I entered the hide. She fed the young again at 10.25, 10.45, and at 11.00. But this time she stayed and sheltered the young from the very hot sun, which was shining straight into the nest. She did not sit on them but stood in the middle of the nest and provided shade with her wings.

Ouzels sheltering young from hot sun — photograph placed in the top 15 by British Birds

Who's going to jump first?

Normally the male would not approach the nest until she left but this time he seemed to realise there was an emergency. At 11.15 he arrived, fed the young underneath the female and then stayed to provide additional shade from the sun. Both birds remained together at the nest for 20 minutes until at 11.35 the sun had moved enough for the shadow of the bank to solve the problem. Whilst in the full sun both parents and all four young had their beaks open to cool themselves exactly as a dog pants in a similar situation.

The photographs I took that day on Ektachrome 200 were of sufficient quality and interest to get one of them placed in the top 15 of the Best Bird Photograph of the Year Competition run by the magazine *British Birds*.

By contrast on 23 May '83 I erected my hide at a nest under a bank by the side of a moorland road not far from Lofthouse in Nidderdale. The four young were fully feathered and probably about 13 days old. Both adults were very agitated and came to within 5 m before I entered the hide at 08.05.

At 08.20 I heard an Ouzel *chook-chooking* and suddenly realised it was one of the young. It was very excited, left the nest and then climbed back into it. There was no sight or sound of the adults. At 08.45 the young adventurer left the nest again, hopped about 15 cm and then returned. Two minutes later the female appeared above the nest and two of the young climbed on to the edge. After a further three minutes, the female called and one young left the nest and hopped about 2 m up the ditch towards both parents, who were *chook-chooking* about 30 m away.

By 09.07 both parents had disappeared and a second young one was preparing to leave the nest. It was preening and flapping its wings vigorously. At 09.30 a very low-flying Tornado howled overhead and frightened the bold young one back into the nest with the other two. (It presumably was not yet inured to the sound as the adults become.)

At 09.34 the male fed all three young and ate three sacs. Five minutes later he fed No. 1, who had left the nest earlier. It then launched itself from the top of the bank and flew about 5 m. At the same time No. 2 left the nest and disappeared out of my view. At 09.50 and 10.07 the male fed Nos 3 and 4 in the nest and at 10.10 No. 3 climbed out. Five minutes later the male returned, fed No. 3 and led it away up the ditch. At 11.45 No. 1 was about 100 m away and No. 4 was still in the nest. Unfortunately at this point I had to leave the site to get back to the office in Harrogate for an appointment! But it was clear that the parents had

actively encouraged the young to leave the nest and led them away from it to a large patch of reeds about 100 m away which provided good cover.

Double broods

Opinions differ on the extent to which Ring Ouzels are double-brooded. Collins *British Birds* states categorically that they are single-brooded, though sometimes a second is reared. Witherby and Bannerman both suggest that second clutches are common but Flegg and Glue question this after analysing some hundreds of nest record cards submitted to the BTO. In my view these are an unreliable source of detailed information as they are usually completed by ornithologists who have no specialist knowledge of this species and have found nests by chance.

To date the most comprehensive field studies that have been published have been made in an area of the Pentland Hills near Loganlea Reservoir by Roger Durman ('73–'77) and Ian Poxton ('79–'84). Their study area was approximately 1.5 km wide and 3 km long, whereas ours is the same width but twice as long.

Table 4 summarises our comparative findings on double broods.

TABLE 4. COMPARATIVE FINDINGS ON DOUBLE BROODS

Source	Number of nesting territories	Number of second broods	Proportion of second broods
Durman, '75–'76	25	11	44%
Poxton, '79–'84	35	17	49%
Appleyard '88–'91	47	29*	62%
Appleyard '91	11	8*	73%

* Plus two third broods.

My figures for '91 do not include two successful third clutches which flew on 20 and 21 July from adjacent territories at the highest part of my study area. Further details of these remarkable performances are described in earlier pages.

In the four-year period '88–'91 my lowest proportion of second clutches was 44 per cent in '89, when I twisted my knee badly and could not visit any territories after 20 June. The highest proportion of second clutches was in '91 with 73 per cent.

There is no doubt in my mind that prior to '91 I stopped looking for second clutches far too early and that the breeding season is much longer than is generally realised. The weather also plays an important part as a lot of rain in late May and June keeps the supply of earthworms at an adequate level to encourage the Ouzels to lay two or even three clutches. June '91 in my study area produced rain almost every day.

A major complication of this subject is that a second clutch may follow a successful first brood or be a replacement for one that has been deserted or predated. Thus the first egg date for second clutches can vary considerably, unlike the first egg dates of first clutches which in my valley tend to be concentrated in the two-week period from 16–30 April. A study of the table on page 33 shows that there are two peaks in May/June. The first, from 11–15 May inclusive, presumably represents replacement clutches and the second, from 26 May–4 June, will be mostly genuine second broods. The earliest recorded date for a genuine second brood was 26 May and the latest 12 June. Both the third clutches had their first egg on 23 June.

Time interval between double broods

A study of the length of the interval (the gap) between the nestlings of the first brood leaving the nest and the laying of the first egg of the second clutch produces some very interesting facts. I have exact timetables (i.e. not estimated) of 13 genuine second clutches, which are shown in the table below.

Meadow Pipit

Skylark with crest raised

TABLE 5											
Interval in days	0	1	2	3	4	5	6	7	8	9	0–9
Total recorded	1	1	0	1	1	2	2	0	3	2	13

The mean gap is 5.5 days. It will be seen that the maximum gap is nine days and the minimum zero which means that the female laid the first egg of the second clutch on the same day that the nestlings of the first clutch left the first nest. In another case the gap was only one day. The gap between a second clutch and a third clutch could only be established at one nest and was five days. So far as replacement clutches are concerned, I have exact dates on only two. These had gaps of seven and eight days respectively, which is within the time spread of ordinary second clutches.

Snow says that in the case of Blackbirds, if there is nothing to disturb the birds' normal routine, the laying of the new clutch usually starts from four to ten days after the ending of the previous nesting attempt. It seems to make no difference whether the previous nesting attempt was successful or not.

It seems probable that the female Ouzel builds the second nest whilst still helping the male to feed the first brood. Otherwise it would not be possible for there to be a gap as short as zero or one day.

This theory is confirmed by two individual cases. On 19 or 20 May '88 three nestlings flew from a nest sheltered by an overhanging rock on a steep slope in a territory we call Ruin. It was only 30 m from a bridleway used by dozens of walkers at weekends. On 20 May a fully constructed but unlined nest was found in a hole in the wall of a ruined building 75 m away from this first nest. By 24 May this had been lined with the usual dead grasses and appeared to be ready for eggs. By Saturday 28 May a little decorative moss had been added to the rim but there were still no eggs and it was the start of the Spring Bank Holiday weekend. When the site was revisited on 1 June both adults were very agitated and the nest had obviously been disturbed — probably by humans. The juveniles of the first brood were flying about in the vicinity.

On 9 June another completely finished nest was found under a rocky outcrop half-way between the first and second nests. When we visited on 11 and 22 June we found no eggs — the adults probably having been put off by the number of hikers using the bridleway.

Another instance of overlapping nests occurred in the territory we call Behind the Hill where we have found nests for nine

Bracken area containing nests for nine consecutive years

consecutive years in an area of bracken-covered hillside of about 0.25 hectares. On 8 May '91 a nest was found with four eggs after a very thorough search of the area. By 20 May the nest contained four eight-day-old nestlings but was predated on that day. All the young were taken and the female was killed; her tail and wing feathers were found beside the nest. On 25 June I returned to the site to check whether another pair had taken over the territory, but it was deserted. However, only 5 m from the first nest I found a second unlined one on a rocky ledge. This had definitely not been there on 8 May when I was searching for the first one.

There seem to be only three possibilities:

1. That the male found a new mate, she built the second nest and then deserted. This seems unlikely as she would probably have rebuilt elsewhere in the territory.
2. That a new pair took over the territory. This seems unlikely as there was no sign of them on 25 June nor again on 3 July when the condition of the second nest was unchanged.
3. Prior to being killed on 20 May the female built her second brood nest, but as was the case at Ruin did not line it.

The third possibility is the most likely bearing in mind the history of the Ruin territory in '88.

It was my intention in '92 to concentrate on this conundrum, but fate intervened. In mid-May when I had a number of sites under intensive observation, I suddenly had to enter hospital for heart surgery. So the theory has still to be proved conclusively — but now with a reconditioned heart and still lots of enthusiasm it may yet be possible! So far as Blackbirds are concerned there is a record from Germany (Berndt '31) of eggs being laid in a new nest while the young were still in the old one.

Durman suggests that after predation a territory is normally vacated by the adults. This does not accord with my findings. Eight pairs of adults whose first clutch was predated remained in the territory and nested again. Two males whose mates were killed on their nests disappeared after a few days from their territories. In three cases of predation I don't know what happened after the first clutch was lost. But it does seem certain that the majority of pairs remain in the same territory and build a second nest there.

Distance between first, second and third brood nests

The mean distance between successful first, second and third brood nests in 26 territories was 64 m and the median 55. The maximum distance apart was 300 m and in four cases the same nest was used twice. In the two cases of third clutches they were 60 and 80 m from their respective second clutches.

I have records of five replacement broods following predation of the first nest and they are not included above. The mean distance in these cases rose to 133 m. The maximum distance apart was 250 m and the minimum 60 m.

TABLE 6. ANALYSIS OF DISTANCES BETWEEN FIRST, SECOND AND THIRD CLUTCHES

Same nest	1–20 m	21–40 m	41–60 m	61–80 m	81–100 m	Above 100 m	TOTAL
4	4	4	3	3	5	3	26

Territories

In the winter months the upper valley is dead and the only birds to be seen are Grouse and the occasional Carrion Crow. The first sign of approaching spring is the appearance of dozens of frogs mating in their small ancestral breeding ponds to which they travel from far and wide every year. This usually takes place during the period 1–14 March.

The Wheatears and the male Ring Ouzels — both coming from North Africa — usually

Wheatear (m)

arrive together with the mean arrival date over six seasons being 25 March. The earliest Ouzel seen in the valley was on 15 March. The female Ouzels arrive after the males and the gap is usually about 7–14 days, although in a late year caused by bad weather they can arrive almost together.

On arrival the males spend the first few days feeding, often in groups of up to four, in the more sheltered areas and then start to establish individual territories.

At the top end of the valley at altitudes between 400 and 500 m, the choice of suitable sites with good cover and adjacent food supplies is very limited. Most of the nests are in heather-covered shakeholes with a few on limestone cliffs. The distance between nests is thus quite large — between 500 and 800 m. There is little open competition for sites — the first male to arrive takes possession and chases off any rival who may come prospecting.

He chooses a commanding point in his territory from which to sing initially — this often being a ruined building, a fence post in a skyline position or the edge of a crag. The date of the first Ouzel song to be heard in the valley is remarkably consistent, as the table shows.

TABLE 7

1992	31 March
1991	6 April
1990	1 April
1989	6 April
1988	4 April

In the middle valley at an altitude of about 300 m there is much more competition for nesting sites and territories. This is where the grassy moorland and bracken meets an area of fields and there is plenty of food available. There are many stone walls, some ruined buildings and a side valley with very steep sides and many boulders.

In '88 a particular study was made of this area to determine what density of Ring Ouzels it was supporting and how the territories were defined. Within a circle with a radius of 200 m at the junction of the two valleys there were five nests with first egg dates lying between 19 April and 6 May. The nearest two nests were 140 m apart, and the rest were each about 200 m from their nearest neighbour. It is interesting to note that Durman states that the recurring minimum distance between occupied nests in his study area was 160–200 m, which correlates closely with my findings. Hems (BWP) quotes a case in Derbyshire where one nest had three others within a distance of 100–300 m.

In my valley a stone wall ran across the centre of the circle and was wholly within the territory of one pair whose nest was in bracken adjacent to it. Throughout the season the other males regularly disputed possession of the wall and often there were three chasing each other up and down and fighting. If the circle were increased to a 400 m radius then two more nests came inside it — making a total of seven. The males at the two outer nests never competed for the central wall but took undisputed possession of other walls from which to sing in their own territories.

It will be seen that the five central nests were contained within an area of only 0.125 km². This is a very high density and much greater than I have found elsewhere. But the conditions at this valley junction are

Middle valley

Very white gorget on older female

ideal for nest concealment, feeding and guarding territories from prominent boulders and walls.

Hosking and Newberry (BWP) reported ten nests in Yorkshire in about 1.3 km² — a density of one nest per 13.0 hectares. In the large circle in my valley there were seven nests in 0.5 km² — a density of one nest per 7.0 hectares. In the smaller circle the density was one nest per 2.5 hectares.

Durman states that in these congested areas a common feeding ground, often up to 400 m from the nest, is frequently used where no aggression has ever been apparent. This exactly accords with the situation at the junction of my two valleys where there is a large damp field grazed by sheep. The area is not disturbed by hikers and is between 150 and 300 m from the central nests whose adults all fed there from time to time. There was never any fighting.

In those parts of the valley where nests may be up to 500 m apart due to a shortage of suitable sites or food, then the territories usually run from one stone wall to another. Early in the season disputes frequently occur along these walls and there is a considerable amount of testing the determination of the males in adjacent territories. The aggressor will fly down towards the centre of his neighbours' territory where a fight will often develop. Eventually the aggressor wearies of the game and allows himself to be chased back to or even over the dividing wall. He may repeat this taunting behaviour a number of times each day, and across a number of his territory boundaries. As most of the males in an area behave in a similar fashion there are considerable flying activities and exchanges of angry calls in late March and April. By the time the young are being fed there is no time or energy available for such diversions and with second nests they hardly ever occur.

In areas where there are no stone walls then other outstanding geographical features may be used as territory markers. These can include large boulders, stunted trees or ruined buildings.

In another part of the Dales, outside my detailed study area, a major A road ascends a rising valley with a very steep heather and boulder covered slope on one side. Across the road there is a less steeply rising patchwork of grassy fields and stone walls with the occasional ruined building. There are two crags at the top end surrounded by heather.

Up to four pairs of Ouzels have colonised this valley in certain years, nesting on both sides of the road but all feeding in the grassy areas. Very heavy articulated trucks and many cars use this route all day but the Ouzels completely ignore them. They fly across the valley not more than 10 m above the traffic when feeding young. I have even watched them collecting food on the grass verges of the road within 1 m of diesel trucks grinding their way to the top of the pass.

The individual territories at this site are ill defined because of the topography. As a result there is a great deal of harassment of neighbours but this never takes place on the communal feeding ground.

During my study of Dippers on the River Wharfe before the War I soon became aware of the fact that certain territories were occupied virtually every year and others only occasionally. I called them A and B sites because there always seemed to be a pair to take over an A site which fell vacant. The most striking example is a bridge which to my personal knowledge has had a nest on it for all save one of the last 50 years. The sequence was only broken then because a water pipe was being laid under the river right alongside the bridge.

My knowledge of Ring Ouzels does not go back as far but certainly one of my territories

Fuel for the long autumn flight. Rowan berries in the lower valley

has been occupied without a break since '79. There are many A category nesting sites in the valley which I can predict from one year to the next with absolute accuracy, even though the birds have been to Africa and back in the meantime!

At the end of the breeding season, some time during July, the importance of territory diminishes. Successful families of Ouzels including juveniles from more than one brood tend to stay together and forage for food over a wide area. On 5 September '81 we watched one such group stripping the juicy red berries from a rowan tree and leaving it denuded after a few hours. In the Yorkshire Dales bilberries are another favourite food in the period during which both young and old are taking on fuel for the long flight to their winter quarters round the Mediterranean and in North Africa.

In the spring and early summer the staple diet of the Ouzels is earthworms of all sizes supplemented by insects when available, including even moths and butterflies.

Predation

In the valley the principal enemies of the Ring Ouzel are foxes, stoats, weasels, Carrion Crows and Magpies. The latter two are principally at the lower end where at the treeline they have more nesting opportunities, but the Crows seem to travel further afield to scavenge. Higher up the degree of predation seems to vary from year to year depending on the amount of time gamekeepers can spend on keeping the number of predators in check.

In early '91 in the valley they had to contend with an absolute plague of rabbits which were destroying the young heather plants and as a result the stoats, in particular, gained the ascendancy. The result was that nine out of 16 Ouzel nests (56 per cent) with eggs or young at altitudes over 350 m were predated

Curlew's nest probably predated by Crows

The gamekeeper

The enemy — Carrion Crow

Retribution — stoat

in '91 whilst in the previous three years only three nests out of 30 (10 per cent) were lost in the same territories.

Throughout the study area '91 was a bad year for predation at all levels — 13 nests being lost out of a total of 21, giving a loss rate of 62 per cent. This compares with a total loss rate amongst 51 nests for the previous three years of 20 per cent.

It is interesting to note that Durman also recorded a loss rate of 20 per cent amongst 64 nests in the Pentland Hills from '73–'77. He suggested that nests with nestlings appeared to be more at risk than those with eggs. However, we have sustained more losses of nests with eggs than with young. But it does appear that nestlings about eight days old are at particular risk. Does a stoat wait to take the brood until they make a good meal but before some of them can escape by leaving the nest?

It has recently been suggested to me that in addition to stoats at the higher altitudes there are also feral ferrets lost by poachers.

The valley usually contains four pairs of nesting Kestrels and without doubt the Ouzels get very concerned about these. We have never seen a Kestrel take a young Ouzel but they invoke a very violent reaction whenever they are in the vicinity of a nest.

Three particular instances spring to mind. At the Ravine on 26 June '90 we were checking on an Ouzel's nest that had contained hatching eggs one week before. As we approached we watched four juvenile Ouzels feeding and then perching on a line of fence posts about 20 m from the nest. Also in the immediate vicinity were two adult Mistle Thrushes, also with four juveniles. Suddenly there was a flurry of activity and noise from the ravine and a female Kestrel emerged from very near the nest. She was being attacked by both adult Ouzels assisted by their juveniles, who were very quickly joined by the whole Mistle Thrush family. The odds were now 12 to 1 and the Kestrel was driven off to perch on the cliff face about 100 m from the nest. The joint attack was then resumed but it took a further ten minutes before the hubbub subsided and the birds dispersed. At this point the female Ouzel visited the nest to check the young, which were unharmed.

On 3 May '89 I was watching a male Ouzel singing on a wall for about five minutes and then feeding in a field nearby for about 30 minutes. Suddenly he flew across a stream to a tree in which he often sang and attacked a male Kestrel on the top branch who tried to grab the Ouzel with his foot as it flew past.

Ouzel (m) after feeding young

The Kestrel flew off but shortly afterwards returned to the Ouzel's other singing tree. The Ouzel attacked again and the Kestrel flew down to the ground in a bracken-covered area. Whilst there he was attacked a further six times in a period of ten minutes until eventually he flew off and sat on a wall whilst the Ouzel sang from the top of a cliff round which all the fighting had taken place.

Unfortunately I had to leave at this point but it occurred to me later that the female Ouzel was probably sitting on a nest either in the bracken or on a bilberry-covered ledge on the cliff and the male was defending her.

A third occasion was on 29 May '89 at the Lower Crag where there was a female Ouzel with two hatching young. A male was in the vicinity getting quite upset at my presence but he suddenly dashed away making very angry alarm calls. About 150 m from the nest a Kestrel was on the ground by a rock. For five minutes he repeatedly attacked it and eventually drove it away. He returned to the nest and stood guard on the heather alongside. About 15 minutes later and about 300 m away I watched a Kestrel, presumably the same one, drop down beside a wall and fly off with some prey in its foot. Upon investigation I found a very bewildered-looking Grouse wandering about looking for one of her chicks which had presumably just been taken.

So it would appear that the aggressive behaviour of the Ring Ouzel *vis-à-vis* Kestrels pays off compared with the more passive reaction of the Grouse.

In some years there are many more Carrion Crows at all levels in the valley than in others. 1987 was one such year. On 8 June I was photographing a nest at the lower Zig-Zag. The Ouzels were both unsettled by the number of Crows in the vicinity and were approaching the nest infrequently and with great caution. At 12.15 two Crows came towards the nest on the ground. The Ouzels let them get to within 5 m and then both of them attacked very aggressively from the air, making very loud *chak-chak* alarm calls. They succeeded in driving them off and I emerged from the hide to clear the whole area of Crows so I could resume photography. The female came back to look around after ten minutes and they were both feeding the young within 20 minutes.

Display, courtship and copulation

When the male Ouzels arrive in their upland breeding areas they are hungry and tired. Many have flown non-stop from the Conti-nent. Their first requirements are food and rest. There is no aggression between them and they can often be seen in groups of three or four. After a few days they scatter in search of individual territories and start to sing from a prominent feature. This singing becomes quite competitive and sallies are made into adjoining territories to establish boundaries. In the Dales these are often walls.

At about this time the females arrive and the whole activity is stepped up. The males become more aggressive and fights quite often develop. These are more ritual than damaging. The opponents face each other and flutter upwards to a height of about 2 m. They raise their feet towards each other and appear to strike at each other with their wings. They flutter up and down together for perhaps a minute and then the aggressor backs off and flies back to his own territory chased by the defender.

On 16 April '91 we watched a display which was unique in our experience. At 10.10 in the Waterfall territory my wife drew my attention to a commotion on the hillside about 30 m above us. Two female Ouzels were fighting each other and a male was with them. They fought in quite a small area (about 10 × 5 m) of short-cropped grass with rocks on it. They started by flying up into the air to a height of about 2–3 m and then fluttering down again. They gradually became more excited and more vigorous. At first they just fluttered their wings in contact with each other but after ten minutes they got really angry. They ascended higher each time, to about 4–5 m, and started using their beaks and claws. All the time they were shrieking at each other. After 15 minutes a clear winner was established and the loser was chased off down valley.

Throughout the encounter the male took no active part but followed the fighting birds at a distance of about 1 m. He looked exactly as if he was acting as umpire. After the fight the winner returned and *chook-chooked* to the male. For 20 minutes they indulged in a courtship display. She pretended to feed but kept moving and stopping whilst he followed some 10–20 m behind. Then the situation reversed and he went ahead pretending to feed and she followed. She *chook-chooked* most of the time but we couldn't ascertain for sure whether he did also. At 10.45 the pair started to feed normally without following each other.

There was no doubt that the fight we watched earlier was a much more serious one than that which takes place between two

Male and female Ouzels look very similar in the rain

males. The females really were battling for possession of the male, which seems to be a complete inversion of the usual situation.

We found the nest of this male and his mate about 75 m away containing five eggs on 3 May. When the young hatched we were able to calculate that the first egg was laid about 21 April. It usually takes three–four days for a female to build a nest so she must have started almost immediately after the fight and courtship on 16 April.

On 23 April we watched another courtship display in the middle of a grassy field about 1 km up the valley from the previous one. At 08.30 a male and female Ouzel played 'follow my leader' in an area about 70 × 50 m. They moved very quickly about 5 m at a time and were separated by about 10–20 m as before. They pretended to feed the whole time. She *chook-chooked* both when she was leading and following. He made a more assertive call, like the *chak-chak* alarm, but infrequently. Twice he chased off intruding males for about 200 m using his full *chak-chak-chak* alarm call, and then he returned to continue the ritual courtship. The two intruders were different birds, one from each of the territories bordering his

own (see p. 60). No copulation was observed and the birds resumed normal feeding after about half an hour. At no time were they nearer to each other than 5 m.

BWP gives details of only one sequence of copulation that has been reported. Korodi Gal says copulation occurs particularly during nest-building and this we can confirm.

We have observed copulation on four occasions. On 29 May '87 at 11.30 a male was singing intermittently from a wall in the Bracken territory for about one hour. During this time a female was feeding on both sides of the wall amongst patches of rushes where it was damp. The male joined her and copulation took place a number of times over a period of about two minutes. Detailed observation was difficult because of the rushes. They then flew into the valley and round in a circle to a cairn upon which the male perched. They were calling to each other in flight.

We found the nest containing four eggs on 8 June about 30 m from where copulation took place. Unfortunately we could not establish the date of the first egg as the nest was predated before the eggs hatched.

On 13 June '87 above Lower Crag we saw a pair copulate three or four times but at long range. This occasion, like the last, would almost certainly be associated with a second brood nest-building.

At 12.30 on 13 May '91 we were watching a female building a nest (described in a previous chapter). After a number of visits to the site with nesting material she appeared on the hillside with some held cross-ways in her beak. The male was in close pursuit. They kept landing, chasing on the ground, taking off again and finally arrived at the nest site. Here the male attempted copulation three times by jumping on her back but she evaded him each time and went into the nest, which was under a rock. He remained outside and watched her from a range of about 0.5 m. After about two minutes she emerged and they flew off together.

At 13.00 on 22 June '91 we were observing at Upper Crag. A male sang from a bank about 15 m from the Range Rover and then disappeared. Very soon a female with a beak full of dry grass stems held sideways appeared in the same place. Suddenly he returned and jumped on her back, beating his wings rapidly. She was in a slight crouch. They copulated three times, each for about five seconds with a ten-second break between. Afterwards she re-arranged her feathers and raised her tail so that the pink vent of her cloaca could be clearly seen. He

Lapwing or Green Plover

flew off, presumably to feed the fledglings of the previous brood who were nearby and she hopped away.

On 25 June we found her nest only 10 m away and were able to establish she had laid her first egg on 23 June, only the day after the copulation we had witnessed (see p. 60). It was in fact the third clutch of this pair.

Birkhead and Moller have recently ('92) published a book called *Sperm Competition in Birds* which explains that male birds like to deposit their sperm as near as possible to the actual egg-laying date in order to reduce the possibility of their mate being fertilised by another male. They also say that 'among wild birds copulation usually ceases once egg laying starts'.

Voice of the Ouzel and sound recording

At the end of March and early April the male Ring Ouzels return. After an initial period of a few days to feed they start to establish their territories by singing. The main song consists of two–five piping notes, with three and four being the most common. The phrase can be written as *pee-pee-pee-pee*. It is repeated over and over again in a monotonous manner and carries for up to 1 km across the moor on a still morning. Individual birds seem to have a preference for singing either three or four note phrases. Two and five notes are exceptional and not repeated for very long.

A four-note phrase lasts for about 1.3 seconds and is then repeated after a gap of about four–five seconds. The whole song may

be quite short but can continue unbroken for five–ten minutes. The details of a complete song of two minutes 28 seconds and containing 36 phrases are shown in Table 8. Occasionally the phrases are interspersed with chuckling, warbling and twittering, but these are at a much lower volume than the principal notes and can only be heard at close range.

TABLE 8.   ANALYSIS OF RING OUZEL SONG RECORDED AT 14.00 HOURS ON 17 JUNE '85 AT THE ZIG-ZAG

Phrase no.	Number of notes per phrase			Elapsed time (minutes/ seconds)
	Normal	Abnormal		
1	5			0.00
2	3			0.05
3	4			0.10
4		5		0.13
5	4			0.17
6	2	1	*	0.21
7	4			0.26
8		3		0.29
9	3			0.32
10	4			0.35
11	4			0.41
12	4			0.46
13		4		0.49
14		4		0.52
15	3			0.55
16		3		0.58
17	4			1.01
18	4			1.05
19	4			1.09
20	4			1.14
21	4			1.19
22	2	1	*	1.24
23	5			1.28
24		3		1.32
25	4			1.36
26		5		1.40
27	4			1.46
28		4		1.51
29	4			1.56
30	5			2.00
31	4			2.05
32		4		2.12
33	5			2.15
34	4			2.20
35	4			2.24
36	4			2.28

Length of song 148 sec.
Total no. of phrases 36

Normal phrases	25
Abnormal phrases	11
Proportion of abnormal phrases	30%

Average spacing of phrases 4.1 sec.

* In phrases number 6 and 22 there were two normal notes and one at a lower frequency (classified abnormal).

On a still morning I have heard as many as five male Ouzels singing at the same time in those areas where the territories are close together. They often counter-sing at each other from one singing post or wall to another. Their main song can also be produced in flight or even on the ground with a beakful of food. Female Ouzels do not sing. The alarm call of a suddenly disturbed or angry male or female Ouzel is a very harsh *chak-chak* or *chak-chak-chak*. As the birds calm down this is replaced by *chook-chook* or *chook-chook-chook* as they keep watch from a nearby vantage point.

Happy Ouzels, particularly females, sometimes produce a series of delightful warm chuckles as they move about their territories.

By contrast, an Ouzel that is worried by, say, the presence of a hide or predator produces a sound exactly like a Robin when one is in the vicinity of its nest. This sound is thin and high-pitched, not loud, and can be expressed as *Seeeee*. It acts as a danger warning to fledglings or to a mate. It has been suggested that it is made at high frequency as it is very difficult for a predator to locate the source of a sound of this nature.

Redshank

Sandpiper

In order to fully appreciate and study the different sounds produced in various situations it is necessary to record them. I use a UHER 4200 Report Monitor for this purpose. This machine is portable and can record and play in stereo using 13 cm reels which can carry 275 m of long play magnetic tape. Recording at a speed of 9.5 cm per second this gives about 45 minutes of recording on each side of the tape. This is the usual tape speed used in wildlife sound recording as it enables the full range of sounds to be accurately reproduced.

In order to amplify sounds coming from some distance it is necessary to use a parabolic reflector in which the microphone is placed. This has the equivalent effect of a telephoto lens on a camera. Mine is an Atherstone with a diameter of 51 cm and amplifies the sound four times. It can either be hand-held or mounted on a tripod. When used on the moors it is almost always necessary to use a cloth baffle over the reflector to minimise wind roar.

As with photography there is a great deal to learn about the art of recording. One can achieve recognisable song quite easily but to get a perfect recording at the correct volume and without interference is another matter. The low-flying aircraft in the vicinity of my valley have ruined many promising tapes of mine, as have the distant voices of hikers blissfully unaware of the fact that I am recording every word they are saying!

Replaying the tapes at home can be very useful when learning all the different sounds the Ouzels make. But much more interesting and valuable use can be made of the tapes by employing a sound spectrograph. This machine analyses the tapes electronically and produces a sonagram. This is a form of graph in which the horizontal scale is time in seconds and the vertical is frequency in cycles per second (Hz). On a black and white sonagram the density of the markings from grey to black represents relative loudness. A single note is therefore broken down into its component parts and presented visually instead of aurally. It is often much easier to compare the visual form of a sound than the sound itself.

A few male Ouzels have the ability to vary the pitch of the notes in phrases as the song progresses. They sing two or three phrases of the normal version and then change to the alternative. They can switch from one version to the other for just one phrase or for a group. Very occasionally they will drop just the last note of a phrase to a lower pitch and then

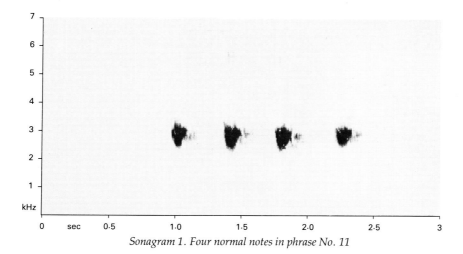

Sonagram 1. Four normal notes in phrase No. 11

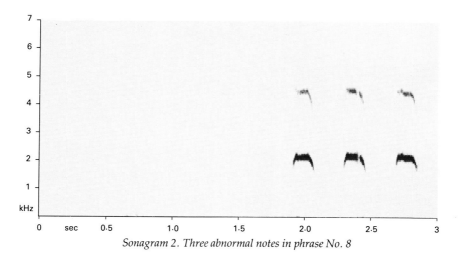

Sonagram 2. Three abnormal notes in phrase No. 8

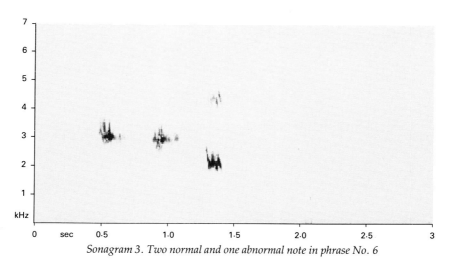

Sonagram 3. Two normal and one abnormal note in phrase No. 6

continue with quite normal ones in the next phrase. An analysis (Table 8) of a complete song illustrating these phenomena is given in this chapter.

It will be seen that on this particular occasion 30 per cent of the phrases produced by the bird were abnormal. The normal note is shown on a sonagram at a frequency of about 3,000 Hz (Sonagram 1). But when an abnormal phrase or single note is introduced it is shown as being composed of two frequencies. The upper one is at about 4,400 Hz and the lower one at 2,200 Hz (Sonagrams 2 and 3). It would seem that the abnormal notes may be produced by the bird, adding a harmonic variation to its repertoire.*

This type of singing by Ouzels is not referred to in any literature that I have seen. I wonder therefore if it is a local phenomenon in the valley comprising my study area. I myself have never heard Ouzels singing in this way elsewhere in the Yorkshire Dales.

*BWP (vol. 1) states that 'Much of the information on a sonagram is not immediately apparent to the ear, e.g. harmonics are not heard as discrete sounds occurring simultaneously but as a single tone with a quality (timbre) which is largely dependent upon the relative strength and distribution of the harmonics.'

BWP (volume 1) describes 'Dialect being produced when there is a tendency among local populations of a species to approximate their songs to a common pattern as a result of mutual imitation'. I estimate that in any given year there are only about four male Ouzels in the valley, out of a total of about eleven, that ever sing in this way. They are all in the area of highest density in the middle valley, where a great deal of counter-singing occurs between males in adjacent territories.

The police use a technique they call 'voice printing' to help them to identify individual criminals or nuisance telephone callers. It is my belief that it is possible to identify individual male Ouzels in the same way. I have many hours of tapes and scores of sonagrams produced in the three-year period '85–'87 which I have not yet had time to analyse fully. But I have done enough work on the subject to satisfy myself that given the time I will be able positively to identify my individual birds from one season to the next. I suggest that a suitable name for this technique would be audio ringing. Research along similar lines has been carried out by Galeotti and Pavan ('91) on the individual recognition of male Tawny Owls.

Ouzel (m) with a tasty morsel

Bird photography and use of video camera

For the photography of shy species, and the Ring Ouzel is certainly that, a hide is essential. It must be possible to transport this easily, erect it quickly and have enough space inside to be able to exist in it for up to seven or eight hours.

My canvas hide is square with sides of 0.8 m and is 1.4 m high. It is supported by collapsible wooden poles with guy-ropes at each corner, and has a pocket all round the bottom to enable the sides to be weighted down with stones to reduce wind shake. In the front is a conical sleeve which conceals the telephoto lens. On all four sides there are observation windows covered with gauze through which the bird cannot see. These also provide ventilation. The final vital piece of equipment is a collapsible fisherman's stool, as squatting for hours on wet peat or a cold rock is not to be recommended. It is essential to have food and copious amounts of liquid.

A hide in full sunshine on a still day becomes like a sauna.

My routine is always to set up the tripod and camera first to ensure that the distance and angles are the best possible. Then the hide is erected over this equipment.

Getting into the hide is another problem. Ideally a second person comes with one and eventually leaves in a conspicuous manner. As birds cannot count they do not realise that the cameraman is still inside and will usually return quite quickly. If one is alone then patience is the only solution until the adults finally return. Even then it is best to wait for two or three visits to enable them to settle down and behave naturally.

With Ouzels one is often helped by the nest being near a stream or by sounds being carried away by the wind. So choosing the right position, bearing in mind also that the sun will move during the day, can be a tricky

Hide in the middle valley

problem. Once ensconced one cannot change anything.

The main difficulty when photographing Ouzels is the wind. It is rarely absent above an altitude of 300 m and causes the canvas sides of the hide to move and crackle. It also makes it virtually impossible to leave a hide unattended overnight as it can easily be blown away.

Very light-breasted female with bulky nest

This means completing the session in one day, which does not give much time for the birds to accept the hide. In practice it was found that about 10 m was the nearest practical distance to be from the nest and even then many Ouzels took up to two hours or more to acclimatise. Nests containing young less than seven/eight days old were never photographed as they needed feathers on their backs to prevent them getting chilled during the waiting period.

Equipment

To obtain satisfactory pictures with good feather detail at a range of 10 m requires at least a 500 mm lens, which gives a magnification ten times that of the standard lens on a 35 mm camera. One is forced to use a mirror type lens to save weight and bulk and also expense. The snag of these lenses is that light-coloured objects in the background produce a doughnut effect in the picture and great care has thus to be taken with the composition.

A Tamron SP 500 mm f8 lens was used for the first three seasons mounted on a Nikon FE camera fitted with motor drive and using automatic aperture priority, i.e. the shutter speed is varied electronically. This facility is essential because on a sunny day with scattered clouds the light intensity can change instantly. With a bird cautiously approaching the nest on the ground one has to refocus continuously and there is no time, nor fingers available, to manually reset the exposure.

But the opportunity arose to acquire second-hand a Nikkor 1,000 mm mirror lens. This had the immediate beneficial effect of being able to retreat to 15 m or more with the hide and still 'appear' to be taking pictures nearer to the nest than before. The advantage was more relaxed adults who returned to the nest much quicker and were less disturbed by the sound of the camera shutter and motor drive. The disadvantage was that at 15 m the depth of focus of a 1,000 mm lens is minimal. This meant that head-on the beak and tail cannot both be in sharp focus and one needed

Ektochrome 400 film, 1000 mm lens, 8 metres distance, steadied only with a monopod at 1/60 sec and f11

exceptional eyesight to refocus quickly as an adult returned to feed the young and the range was changing all the time. Another snag was that a mirror lens has a fixed aperture. In the case of the Nikkor 1,000 mm this was f11 and thus the only variants one was left with were shutter speed and film speed.

Types of film

It is generally accepted that the best colour slide film for bird photography is Kodachrome with an ISO rating of 64. But at f11 this is only usable in very good lighting conditions as, ideally, to freeze a nervous bird at the nest requires an exposure time shorter than 1/100 second. Kodak have recently produced Kodachrome 200, which helps to overcome this problem and for many years their Ektochrome 200 has been available, with ISO 400 added a few years ago.

But on days with heavy cloud and rain a much faster film has to be used. Fuji have recently introduced a colour slide film with a much higher rating of 1600 but I have no personal experience of it yet. Consequently I have often been forced to use colour print film which has been available for some years from a number of makers at ratings as high as 3200. But at this upper level it is only worth using if one is trying to get some record of an unrepeatable incident in impossibly low lighting conditions.

Most of my photographs have been taken using either 400 or 1600 film and a very sturdy tripod. There is at last one available, a Benbo, which is not only immensely strong but can easily be adjusted to conform to any configuration of ground or rocks. The penalty for its versatility is weight but it has enabled me to take good pictures of birds at the nest with a 1,000 mm f11 lens using ISO 400 film at shutter speeds as low as 1/30 second. The trick is to take two shots in succession as quickly as the motor drive will allow. The bird freezes when it hears the camera the first time and is thus absolutely still for the second.

Taking good photographs of Ouzels is difficult. It is fairly easy to get a recognisable picture of a male showing his white gorget and the rest of him looking black. But to get perfect feather definition and colour all over is another matter. In direct sunlight it is virtually impossible because the white 'burns out'

and the light reflects from the shiny black feathers. The perfect conditions are a lightly overcast sky throwing no shadows and only a light wind. A difficult combination to achieve on a Yorkshire moor at 500 m!

The biggest lesson I have learned is always to carry a lot of films, both transparency and print, in many different ISO ratings and in 36 exposure rolls. It is then possible to cope with a day of varying lighting conditions without the frustrating experience of running out of usable film just as something exciting is starting to happen.

As a result I often shoot over 200 exposures in a day. But really the cost of film is negligible compared with the effort and cost of being there. To get all the photographic and sound recording equipment across moorland tracks requires the use of a 4 × 4 vehicle and that needs the permission and help of the land owner, farmers, shepherds and gamekeepers. We have been very fortunate to receive this over the years and we are very grateful.

Use of video camera

During my Ouzel study I have amassed thousands of photographs, all in colour, both in

Female below nest and ignoring video camera

slide and print form. But each one shows only what was happening at one precise moment in time. To obtain a continuous detailed record of general behaviour in and around the nest a cine-camera is required but this has two disadvantages. Film is now prohibitively expensive and the camera has to be operated from a hide because of the need to change the film from time to time.

It occurred to me that by using a video camera one could overcome this objection and obtain a number of advantages. I now use a Nikon VN–7000 which operates on 8 mm tapes. These can be obtained in a length which runs for 90 minutes continuously when the camera is powered by a recharge-able battery with a life of about two hours. The whole unit is about the size of one's hand and weighs just over 1 kg with battery. It has an eight times zoom lens and fully automatic operation but can be operated manually including the aperture. It runs silently.

Consequently I mount it on a tripod at a range of about 2.5 m from the nest, zoom the lens to the required magnification, set it run-ning and go away. The aperture changes automatically with the lighting conditions, the focus changes as the bird moves position and the built-in microphone records all sounds in the vicinity. On the first occasion I was concerned that the Ouzels might not accept the camera so near but there was no need to worry. When I walked away and turned round from about 50 m it was to see one of the birds actually standing on the leg of the tripod! The technique has the great advantage that the birds behave quite natur-ally the whole time and are not disturbed by any sounds from a shutter or the hide.

In contrast to a cine-film one can see and hear the result on a television set as soon as one gets home, and if necessary return the next day to obtain an improved performance. In the chapter giving details of behaviour at the nest these video films have been invalu-able because of course the exact time of every-thing that happens can be calculated so long as the starting time is noted. The films can be run and re-run as many times as is necessary to write down exactly what has happened, compared with trying to do the same in a hide during the course of the action.

The abandoned farm in the upper valley — now the home of the Kestrels

'On Curlew-haunted moor'

In memoriam

In July '43 the author's elder brother, Major Geoffrey Appleyard, DSO, MC and Bar, was killed leading an SAS airborne attack on the bridges north of Taormina in Sicily. He was 26 years of age. Their father wrote a book in his memory from which the following passage is taken:

> Although he may not come back he never seems far away. Often indeed he seems very near; not least so when we are tramping over his beloved Yorkshire fells, the wind carrying the varied sounds of the moorland — the splash of a nearby stream, the whisper of the long grass, the bleating of lambs and suddenly, the lovely, bubbling cry of a Curlew — the bird he loved above all others. Then we recall what Geoffrey said one day as the same call came faintly across the moor: 'That's how I'd like to return to earth when my time comes.'

It seems appropriate that this Ouzel story should conclude with a poem which might have been written for the author and his brother.

> On summer hill, in greenwood quick with Spring,
> On Curlew-haunted moor and rocky shore,
> Your loved, long-silent voice is heard no more
> Nor anywhere your clear, low whistling;
> And yet I think your voice has taken wing
> For when to morning skies the brown larks soar
> Or when from evening trees song medleys pour,
> I hear your voice again — remembering
> The woods of childhood where, beloved guide,
> You taught my questing mind and eager ear
> The lore of birds — a story without end.
> Remembering day-long rambles by your side.
> And now I go about the world and hear
> Your voice in all birds' songs and count them friend.
>
> *Helen B. G. Sutherland*

Glossary

Some of the definitions used have been taken from *The Bird Watcher's Dictionary* by Peter Weaver, to whom grateful acknowledgement is made.

Albino	Albinism is caused by lack of melanin pigmentation. A fully albino bird has white feathers and pink eyes. It is thought to come from a deficiency in diet.
Bents	Dried stalks of slender grass.
Bothy	A Scottish name for a one-roomed hut or cottage.
Chak-chak	Alarm call of a suddenly disturbed Ouzel.
Chook-chook	Worried call of an Ouzel if one is too near a nest.
Counter-singing	Alternation of song which may occur when two or more territory holders are responding to one another (BWP).
Distraction display	A bird feigning injury to lead a predator away from a nest or young.
Doline	See Shakehole.
Faecal sac	A white jelly-like 'envelope' in which the faeces of nestlings is enclosed.
Fledgling	A young bird that has just left the nest.
f stop	The size of the lens aperture on a camera is called an f stop, e.g. f8 and f11. The latter lets through only half as much light as the former.
g	Gram (0.0353 ounces).
Gorget	A zone of colour across the breast of a bird. Also known as a pectoral band. Takes the form of white crescent on the male Ring Ouzel.
Hectare	100 hectares equal 1 km². 1 hectare equals 2.471 acres.
Hz	Cycles per second.
ISO	A rating of the sensitivity or speed of a film.
Juvenile	A young bird in its first covering of feathers.
Karst scenery	An area of weathered limestone similar to the Karst region of the former Yugoslavia.
kg	Kilogram (2.2046 pounds); includes 1,000 grams.
km	Kilometre (0.6214 mile); includes 1,000 metres.
km²	Square kilometre.
m	Metre (3.28 feet).
Mean	The average of a set of figures calculated by summing them and then dividing the sum by the number of figures.
Median	If a set of figures is ranked in order the middle one is called the median.
Nestling	A young bird in the nest.
Nest record cards	Completed in great detail by ornithologists all over Britain in respect of nests found during a season.
Nidiculous	Young that hatch in an undeveloped state (i.e. Ring Ouzels). They remain in the nest for a period, completely dependent on parental care.
Nidifugous	Young that hatch in a relatively developed state and leave the nest almost immediately. Sometimes called 'downies'.
O.P.	Observation point.
Pointer	A breed of dog that 'points' when it discovers game.
Pothole	Entrance to an underground cave system.
Predated	Destroyed by a predator.
Predation	The activity of predators.
Predator	An animal or bird which feeds on other animals, birds or eggs.
SAS	Special Air Service Regiment.

Schedule I	A list of rare birds afforded special protection under the law from interference of any kind.
Shakehole	Swallow-hole, sink or doline — a hole down which surface waters proceed underground in limestone country.
Skyline peeping	The habit of male Ouzels keeping watch on an intruder by popping their heads over the skyline from time to time.
Sleeping	The habit of male Ouzels appearing to sleep, but with their eyes open, when on watch near the nest.
Sonagram	A visual representation of sound, in the form of a trace on a graph, in which the vertical axis shows frequency (pitch), being graduated in Kilo Hertz (Kilocycles) and the horizontal axis shows duration (in seconds). The machine used is called a sonagraph or sound-spectrograph.
Tell-tale	Extraneous material attached to the rim of a nest, e.g. a length of sheep-wool or a dead bracken stem.
Territory	The defended area in which a pair of Ouzels breeds during the course of one season. They may rear one, two or even three broods within its boundaries. It is rigorously guarded, particularly by the male.
Treeline	The altitude beyond which trees are unable to grow because of the climatic conditions in the area.
Upland	The area of grass and heather moor lying roughly between 240 and 600 m above sea level.

Timetable

1–14 March	The season commences with the return of the frogs to their ancestral breeding ponds.
15 March	Earliest recorded arrival of a male Ouzel.
25 March	Average arrival date of males.
26 March	Earliest arrival of a female.
31 March	Earliest song.
13 April	Earliest egg.
22 April	Average earliest egg over 13 seasons.
21–30 April	Peak period for laying of first egg.
11–15 May	Peak period for replacement clutches.
26 May–4 June	Peak period for second clutches.
23 June	First egg of a third clutch (two territories).
12 August	Start of Grouse shooting season.
August–September	Family groups roaming the uplands for berries and other food.
Mid-September	Ouzels start leaving to begin their long autumn flight to their wintering areas around the Mediterranean.
October	The other upland birds have left this hostile environment leaving only the Grouse to exist there throughout the winter.

References

BLOWS British Library of Wildlife Sounds, National Sound Archive.

BTO British Trust for Ornithology.

Bannerman, D. A. 1954 *The Birds of the British Isles*.

BWP 1988 *The Birds of the Western Palearctic*, volume 5. Oxford University Press.

Birkhead, T. R. and Moller, A. P. 1992 Sperm Competition in Birds. Academic Press.

Berndt, R. 1931 'Ineinandergeschachtelte Bruten der Amsel (Turdus m. merula L.)', *Orn. Monatsb.*, 39, 152.

Durman, Roger F. 1976 'Ring Ouzel Migration', *Bird Study*, vol. 23, no. 3.

Durman, Roger F. 1977 Edinburgh Ringing Group Report No. 5, 24–27.

Flegg, J. J. M. and Glue, D. E. 1975 'The Nesting of the Ring Ouzel', *Bird Study*, vol. 22, part 1, 1–8.

Galeotti, P. and Pavan, G. 1991 'Individual Recognition of Male Tawny Owls (Stix aluco) Using Spectrograms of their Territorial Calls', *Ethology, Ecology and Evolution*, 3: 113–26.

Hems, H. A. 1966 *British Birds*, 59, 107–08.

Hosking, E. and Newberry, C. W. 1946 *More Birds of the Day*.

Korodi Gal, J. 1965 *Zool. Abh. Staatl.* Mus. Tierkde, Dresden.

Mather, John R. 1986 *The Birds of Yorkshire*. Croom Helm.

Poxton, Ian R. 1986 'Breeding Ring Ouzels in the Pentland Hills', *Scottish Birds*, 14, 44–48.

Poxton, Ian R. 1987 'Breeding Status of the Ring Ouzel in Southeast Scotland 1985–86', *Scottish Birds*.

Reader's Digest 1986 *Field Guide to the Birds of Britain*.

Sharrock, J. T. R. 1976 *The Atlas of Breeding Birds in Britain and Ireland*. BTO.

Snow, D. W. 1988 *A Study of Blackbirds*. British Museum (Natural History).

Simms, Eric. 1978 *British Thrushes*. Collins.

Witherby, H. F. 1938 *The Handbook of British Birds*. H. F. & G. Witherby.

Weaver, Peter. 1981 *Bird Watcher's Dictionary*. T. & A. D. Poyser.

Postscript

Since finishing this book I have re-read 'A Study of Blackbirds' by D. W. Snow (1988). In this he sheds more light on two of the behavioural problems which have puzzled me.

(a) *Ouzels and Blackbirds*

I describe the unusually close association between male Ouzels and male Blackbirds at the beginning of the season on Page 16.

 Snow says that in the autumn many of our Blackbirds who have bred in the north of England migrate westwards to Ireland and return in the spring. Could those early companions of the Ouzels be such birds? They do not have mates and presumably drop down to the lower levels below the treeline to find one when the female Ouzels start to return to the higher ground.

(b) *Copulation*

The timing of copulation between Ouzels is recorded on Pages 31 and 48. The interference of other males from neighbouring territories is described on Page 47.

 Snow has this to say about Blackbirds whose courtship rituals are similar to those of Ouzels.

'Females solicit copulation for only a short period at the beginning of each nesting cycle: five observed copulations of colour-ringed females took place from one to five days before the laying of their first egg.

 The sight of a pair copulating or about to copulate has an immediate and powerful effect on neighbouring males. In nearly every case that I observed, copulations were interfered with by the sudden arrival of one or two males, who either knocked the copulating male off the female or prevented him from mounting. And these attacks have been directed against a territory-holder in the middle of his own territory, where the neighbours normally never go or, if they do, only with every sign of nervousness. Probably because of this habitual interference, copulation is a very brief business lasting only a few seconds.'

Two of my own observations of Ouzels either attempting or achieving copulation produced gaps of one day and two days between the act and the first egg being laid. This accords exactly with the Blackbird data.